The Most Important Meetings of the Allies during World War II: The History of the Tehran Conference, Yalta Conference, and Potsdam Conference

By Charles River Editors

Churchill, Roosevelt, and Stalin at the Yalta Conference

About Charles River Editors

Charles River Editors provides superior editing and original writing services across the digital publishing industry, with the expertise to create digital content for publishers across a vast range of subject matter. In addition to providing original digital content for third party publishers, we also republish civilization's greatest literary works, bringing them to new generations of readers via ebooks.

Sign up here to receive updates about free books as we publish them, and visit Our Kindle Author Page to browse today's free promotions and our most recently published Kindle titles.

Introduction

Stalin and Roosevelt at Tehran

The Tehran Conference

"We are sitting around this table for the first time as a family, with the one object of winning the war. [...] In such a large family circle we hope that we will be very successful and achieve a constructive accord in order that we may maintain close touch throughout the war and after the war." - Prime Minister William Churchill to President Franklin Roosevelt, Soviet premier Josef Stalin, and others at the Tehran Conference, November 28th, 1943

Separated by vast gulfs of political, cultural, and philosophical divergence, the three chief Allied nations of World War II – the United States, the Soviet Union, and Great Britain – attempted to formulate a joint policy through a series of three conferences during and immediately after the conflict.

The first meeting took place in Tehran in late 1943, while the fate of World War II still hung in the balance. The fate of World War II hung in the balance in 1943. On the Eastern Front, the opposed juggernauts of the Wehrmacht, army of Adolf Hitler's Third Reich, and the Red Army, the military force of Josef Stalin's Soviet Union, grappled in a nearly apocalyptic battle. Black smoke rose into the steppe air from burning vehicles strewing the landscape, while millions of men maneuvered, fought, and died in a series of brutal encounters. Meanwhile, the Western Allies succeeded in ousting the Germans from North Africa, then took Sicily with Operation Husky and landed in Italy. There, the tough, hardened warriors of the German military turned the Italian peninsula into a vast fortress; these seasoned fighters made the determined Anglo-American forces pay a bitter price for each mountain ridge, river crossing, and stony valley swept by cunningly-placed gun emplacements.

Half a world away, in the Pacific, the Americans finally halted the Japanese expansion across the ocean, but the Empire of the Rising Sun refused to give up the ghost just yet. An Allied effort to invade Burma came to grief, while the Imperial Japanese Army (IJA) struggled with the Chinese in massive land battles, used biological warfare against the civilian population, and faced a situation not unlike Hitler's in Russia.

Nearing the end of the year, with the Axis halted but still terrifyingly powerful, and the fortunes of war appearing likely to swing either way, the Allies deemed it necessary for their leaders to meet, coordinating their war planning. Feelers for a conference went out from President Roosevelt as early as 1942, but profound differences between the purposes of the various Allies already appeared at that time. Stalin, in particular, wanted territorial gains for the Soviet Union, already looking hungrily at Poland, a notable ally of the Western powers. Accordingly, FDR reached out to Stalin for both cooperation and a summit: "Such a meeting of minds in personal conversation would be greatly useful in the conduct of the war against Hitlerism. Perhaps if things go as well as we hope, you and I could spend a few days together next summer near our common border off Alaska. But in the meantime, I regard it as of the utmost military importance that we have the nearest possible approach to an exchange of views." (Eubank, 1985, 46).

Though made in April 1942, this proposal bore no fruit until late November 1943, in a location far from the Alaskan venue Roosevelt envisioned. Stalin showed little hurry to meet with his allies, whom he deeply distrusted and viewed only as tools for advancing Soviet interests. Thus, when the Big Three – FDR, Winston Churchill, and Josef Stalin – finally met, it would be in the dusty, half-medieval streets of Iran's capital, Tehran, about 6,400 miles from American shores.

At Tehran in November 1943, Stalin was at a disadvantage. He was something like the out of town stranger that someone had brought home for Thanksgiving Dinner. England and America were related both ethnically and politically. They also spoke the same language, ate the same sorts of foods and shared a mutual history going back nearly 1,000 years. Russia, on the other hand, was a mystery, a separate entity steeped in archaic tradition and mystery. Therefore, Stalin could not help but feel like an outsider.

Still, Stalin had no problem holding his own when it came time to talk of military strategy. Lord Alan Brooke, a British Field Marshall and Churchill's aid, kept a lengthy diary of the conference, and this is how he described Stalin: "During this meeting and all the subsequent ones which we had with Stalin, I rapidly grew to appreciate the fact that he had a military brain of the very highest calibre. Never once in any of his statements did he make any strategic error, nor did he ever fail to appreciate all the implications of a situation with a quick and unerring eye. In this respect he stood out compared with his two colleagues."

Ultimately, Stalin sided with Roosevelt and pressured the British into accepting a cross-channel invasion of France for the following year. Churchill was reluctantly forced to recognize that Britain had become the junior partner in the enterprise.

Over 70 years later, the Tehran Conference is not as well known as the two major conferences that came after it – Yalta and Potsdam – but it had a profound influence in shaping the course of the rest of the war. While the conference took care of peripheral matters related to the region, particularly Turkey and Iran, and it touched upon the topics of fighting Japan and shaping the post-war world, the conference was most notable for its agreement to open up a second front against Nazi Germany in Western Europe, which even the Nazis figured would almost certainly take place somewhere in Vichy France. As a result, Tehran was instrumental in the coming operations that culminated with the D-Day invasion on June 6, 1944 and the rest of Operation Overlord.

The Most Important Meetings of the Allies during World War II: The History of the Tehran Conference, Yalta Conference, and Potsdam Conference looks at the crucial conference and its results, most notably the preparations for D-Day the following year. Along with pictures of important people, places, and events, you will learn about the Tehran Conference like never before.

The Yalta Conference

Churchill, Roosevelt, and Stalin at the Yalta Conference

"Do you think they will stop just to please you, or us for that matter? Do you expect us and Great Britain to declare war on Joe Stalin if they cross your previous frontier? Even if we wanted to, Russia can still field an army twice our combined strength, and we would just have no say in the matter at all." – President Franklin D. Roosevelt to the Polish ambassador in Washington, D.C. (Gardner, 1993, 208-209).

Adolf Hitler's Third Reich had scant time remaining when the "Big Three" met at the Yalta Conference in February 1945 to discuss the future of Germany, Europe, and the postwar world as a whole. No doubt existed regarding the war's outcome; the Americans had shattered the Wehrmacht's desperate last throw in the west, the Ardennes Offensive, during the Battle of the Bulge in the weeks immediately preceding Yalta, and the Soviet front lay just 50 miles east of Berlin, with the Red Army preparing for its final push into the Reich's capital after a successful surprise winter campaign.

Among the agreements, the Conference called for Germany's unconditional surrender, the split of Berlin, and German demilitarization and reparations. Stalin, Churchill and Roosevelt also discussed the status of Poland, and Russian involvement in the United Nations. By this time

Stalin had thoroughly established Soviet authority in most of Eastern Europe and made it clear that he had no intention of giving up lands his soldiers had fought and died for. The best he would offer Churchill and Roosevelt was the promise that he would allow free elections to be held. He made it clear, though, that the only acceptable outcome to any Polish election would be one that supported communism. One Allied negotiator would later describe Stalin's very formidable negotiating skills. "Marshal Stalin as a negotiator was the toughest proposition of all. Indeed, after something like thirty years' experience of international conferences of one kind and another, if I had to pick a team for going into a conference room, Stalin would be my first choice. Of course the man was ruthless and of course he knew his purpose. He never wasted a word. He never stormed, he was seldom even irritated."

The final question lay in what to do with a conquered Germany. Both the Western Allies and Stalin wanted Berlin, and knew that whoever held the most of it when the truce was signed would end up controlling the city. Thus they spent the next several months pushing their generals further and further toward this goal, but the Russians got there first. Thus, when the victorious allies met in Potsdam in 1945, it remained Britain and America's task to convince Stalin to divide the country, and even the city, between them. They accomplished this, but at a terrible cost: Russia got liberated Austria.

Given its context and importance, the Yalta Conference represented a contentious matter in its own day, and it remains so among historians both professional and amateur. As just one example, while some lauded Roosevelt's political dexterity, many others viewed him as excessively naïve in his dealings with Stalin, or even as a pro-communist quisling.

Furthermore, while the representatives of the chief Allied powers made important decisions at Yalta, they did not divide Europe at that time. The exact future of Europe remained fluid, only coalescing in a more familiar Cold War form during and after the Potsdam Conference following Germany's defeat. In fact, the actual strategic situation, with its iron, deterministic logic of military power, cut across the hopes and intentions of the participants. The West wanted Eastern Europe freed and democratic once again, but Stalin already owned it and mustered hundreds of divisions to enforce his ownership. The Russians wanted Germany but the Anglo-American offensive would likely engulf most of it before the Soviets broke through the final defenses of the dying Wehrmacht.

Thus, the Yalta Conference proved mostly futile, with the sole exception of establishing the United Nations, at Roosevelt's insistence. The nine agreements that Stalin, Churchill, and Roosevelt signed at the end of the Conference used trumpeting phrases about freedom, peace, and brotherhood, but they contained no practical or actionable content. These documents temporarily papered over the fact that the shape of postwar Europe would be decided not by reasoned arguments, but by the fierce, undeniable logic of shells, bullets, tanks, and aircraft.

Yalta neither delayed nor created the Cold War; the collision between two utterly incompatible systems of thought – one that, despite its flaws, placed its faith in freedom, human rights, and majority rule, and the other that believed in paranoid dictatorship enforced through systematic state violence and terror – seemed inevitable either way. If anything, Yalta enabled the three leaders to project a momentary phantasm of unity, permitting them to postpone their intractable hostility for a few months in order to first defeat Germany.

The Most Important Meetings of the Allies during World War II: The History of the Tehran Conference, Yalta Conference, and Potsdam Conference looks at the controversial conference and its results. Along with pictures of important people, places, and events, you will learn about Yalta like never before.

The Potsdam Conference

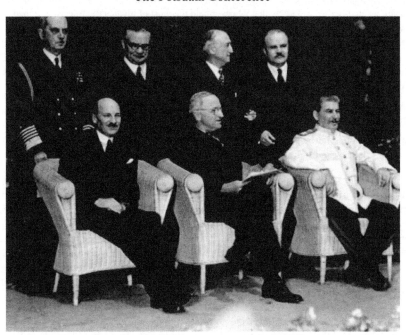

Attlee, Truman, and Stalin at the Potsdam Conference

"If we can put this tremendous machine of ours, which has made this victory possible, to work for peace, we can look forward to the greatest age in the history of mankind. That's what we propose to do." - President Harry S. Truman at a July 1945 flag-raising ceremony in Berlin

Standing in history like a milestone marking the boundary between one era and the next, the Potsdam Conference brought together the leaders of the three major Allied powers – the United States, the Soviet Union, and the United Kingdom – for the last time at the end of World War II and at the threshold of the Cold War. A follow up to the Yalta Conference just five months earlier, Potsdam attempted to work out the contours of the postwar world.

Though it came so shortly after Yalta, the Potsdam Conference also highlighted a turnover of leadership on the world stage. British Prime Minister Winston Churchill, who gave his nation hope in the darkest days of World War II, had suffered a stunning defeat at the hands of the Labor candidate Clement Attlee, who replaced him towards the end of the Conference. President Franklin Delano Roosevelt died prior to the meeting, leading to his replacement by the new president Harry S. Truman, a keen-minded pragmatist whose intense focus on America's advantage contrasted with Roosevelt's internationalism. Only General Secretary Josef Stalin, dictator of the Soviet Union, remained unchanged from the earlier summit. Destined to continue in power for another 8 years until his death (possibly at the hands of Lavrenty Beria), the Russian strongman found himself confronting a world in which the United States possessed the atomic bomb.

At the same time, despite the power of the central personalities, their lieutenants also played a role at Potsdam. James Byrnes, Truman's right-hand man at the conference, concealed a deeply astute, intelligent, and cunning mind under the exterior of a scrawny country bumpkin. Fleet Admiral William D. Leahy provided continuity with the Yalta conference for the American delegation, while Vyacheslav Molotov and Foreign Minister Anthony Eden also reprised their roles from the earlier summit.

World War II was so horrific that in its aftermath, the victorious Allies sought to address every aspect of it to both punish war criminals and attempt to ensure that there was never a conflict like it again. World War II was unprecedented in terms of the global scale of the fighting, the number of both civilian and military casualties, the practice of total war, and war crimes. World War II also left two undisputed, ideologically opposed superpowers standing, shaping global politics over the last 65 years.

Though the countries had often discussed Russia joining America and Britain's fight against the Japanese, it became clear at Potsdam that this was not going to happen. Instead, Stalin pleaded for help for his own country, which had been decimated by the fighting with Germany. Russia had lost more than 30,000 factories and so much farm land that the vast majority of the population was suffering from malnutrition. Stalin was also particularly concerned that the Allies might stage an invasion of Russia and overthrow his regime. While it may have seemed at the time that he was just being paranoid, it is now known that George Patton was already pushing Truman and the other world leaders to go ahead and finish the weakened Soviets off, meaning Stalin might actually have been wise to build up communist governments in Czechoslovakia,

East Germany, Bulgaria and elsewhere.

The British and Americans didn't see it that way, though. Instead, they assumed that Stalin was expanding the Soviet Union in preparation for invading Europe. The Europeans appealed to the Americans for help and with them would go on to create the North Atlantic Treaty Organization in 1949. This mutual mistrust among all parties involved marked the beginning of the Cold War.

The Most Important Meetings of the Allies during World War II: The History of the Tehran Conference, Yalta Conference, and Potsdam Conference looks at the final major conference of the war and its results. Along with pictures of important people, places, and events, you will learn about the Potsdam Conference like never before.

The Most Important Meetings of the Allies during World War II: The History of the Tehran Conference, Yalta Conference, and Potsdam Conference

The Tehran Conference

Chapter 1: The Road to Tehran

Entering 1943, the Allies looked to press their advantage in the Pacific and Western Europe. The United States was firmly pushing the Japanese back across the Pacific, while the Americans and British plotted a major invasion somewhere in Western Europe to relieve the pressure on the Soviets, who had just lifted the siege of Stalingrad. The Allies were now firmly winning the war. From January 14th to the 24th of 1943, Roosevelt, Churchill and other Allied leaders met in Casablanca, Morocco, but Stalin declined so that he could stay back and manage affairs in Stalingrad. The Casablanca Conference set out Allies demands for an unconditional surrender of Axis Powers. The leaders also agreed to the first major allied assault on Europe: an invasion from North Africa via Sicily into Germany. Roosevelt also agreed to increase submarine bombing in the Atlantic and to send more aid to the Soviet Union

The Allies now had the potential to invade Western Europe or even use North Africa from which to launch an invasion, meaning the Germans had to prepare for several contingencies. And despite fighting in North Africa and the Atlantic, the United States still had the manpower and resources to cripple the Japanese at the Battle of Midway, the first naval battle ever fought in which both navies were never in sight of each other. For their part, the Russians had destroyed an entire German army at Stalingrad by February 1943, and Hitler's Russian invasion had passed its apex.

Stalingrad proved to be Germany's high water-mark against the Soviet Union. For the rest of the war, they were in a constant state of retreat. As the Red Army chased them out and retook more and more of the countryside, they were appalled by the treatment both soldiers and civilians had received at the German's hands. Over four million Soviet prisoners of war had died of starvation, sickness and other forms of mistreatment. In continuation of the "Final Solution," they had also killed all the Jews they captured, as well as civilians of any other ethnic group Hitler didn't care for. It seems that their thought process was that the more Soviet people they killed, the fewer they'd have to deal with later. It has been estimated that the invading Nazis completely razed over 10,000 Russian villages to the ground, slaughtering all the inhabitants they could get their hands on.

As word of German genocide spread throughout the Soviet Union it had a galvanizing rather than weakening effect. Instead of surrendering to the invading forces in hopes of receiving fair treatment, the Soviet peasants would hide in the woods when they heard of an approaching German army. From there, they would organize guerrilla groups that would strike at the Germans from all angles, picking off sentries, disrupting supply lines and spreading chaos. Likewise, the Russian soldier knew that he had a better chance of survival in the field of battle than if they were taken prisoner, so they were more than willing to fight to the death.

Following the victory at Stalingrad, Stalin was gratified to be invited to join Churchill and Franklin Delano Roosevelt at a secret conference in Teheran in November 1943. Once ostracized by the now disgraced Chamberlain, Stalin must have felt vindicated as he sat down as a member of "The Big Three." However, his pleasure was short lived as Churchill and Roosevelt once more denied his request that the allies immediately open up a second front to drive the Germans out of Western Europe. Unfortunately Stalin's own success at Stalingrad had demonstrated that England and the United States were not as necessary to Soviet survival as Stalin had once claimed.

For the Allied leaders, the main strategic issue became that of the so called Second Front. Where would the main effort of the Western Allies be in 1944? The first tensions with Roosevelt on this subject arose in Quebec, in August 1943. It had been hard work to convince the Americans of the merits of an invasion of Sicily. Now Churchill was sure that an Italian campaign was the key to defeating Germany.

The British and Americans debated over their next course of action, with the British favoring an invasion of Sicily over the skepticism of the Americans, who believed the operation was overly ambitious and not a direct enough strike against Hitler's Germany. Eventually the British won out by arguing that invading and controlling Sicily would give the Allies a free hand across the Mediterranean Sea, facilitating both commerce and transportation. Since the invasion would be made by the 7th U.S. Army (led by Patton) and the British 8th Army (led by Montgomery), the soldiers in the North African theater, the operation fell under the overall command of Eisenhower.

In July 1943, less than half a year after the surrender at Stalingrad, the Allies conducted what at the time was the largest amphibious invasion in history, coordinating the landing of two whole armies on Sicily over a front more than 100 miles long. Within a month, the Allies had taken control of the entire island, setting in motion a chain of events that led to Italy quitting the war and Mussolini being hanged. Though Italy was no longer fighting for the Axis, German forces continued to occupy and control Italy in 1943. The Germans attempted to resist the Allies' invasion on Sicily but were badly outmanned and outgunned, leading to a German evacuation of the island within a month. The Allies would land on the mainland of Italy in September and continue to campaign against the Germans there.

Meanwhile, Stalingrad proved to be Germany's high water-mark against the Soviet Union. For the rest of the war, they would find themselves unable to push forward, and eventually find themselves in a constant state of retreat. As the Red Army chased them out and retook more and more of the countryside, they were appalled by the treatment both soldiers and civilians had received at the German's hands. Over four million Soviet prisoners of war had died of starvation, sickness and other forms of mistreatment. In continuation of the "Final Solution," they had also killed all the Jews they captured, as well as civilians of any other ethnic group

Hitler didn't care for. It seems that their thought process was that the more Soviet people they killed, the fewer they'd have to deal with later. It has been estimated that the invading Nazis completely razed over 10,000 Russian villages to the ground, slaughtering all the inhabitants they could get their hands on.

As word of German genocide spread throughout the Soviet Union, it had a galvanizing rather than weakening effect. Instead of surrendering to the invading forces in hopes of receiving fair treatment, the Soviet peasants would hide in the woods when they heard of an approaching German army. From there, they would organize guerrilla groups that would strike at the Germans from all angles, picking off sentries, disrupting supply lines and spreading chaos. Likewise, the Russian soldier knew that he had a better chance of survival in the field of battle than if they were taken prisoner, so they were more than willing to fight to the death.

It was against the backdrop of these military events that posturing and behind the scenes communications between the leaders would bring about the Tehran Conference. Also known by the codename of the Eureka Summit, the conference came about only through labyrinthine negotiations between Churchill, Roosevelt, and Stalin. Letters and telegrams flew thickly between the leaders, envoys came and went, and smaller talks and negotiations wrangled on for months before the two chief Western leaders finally coaxed the coy eastern dictator to meet them face to face.

Roosevelt keenly desired to advance his idea for opening a second front in Western Europe through the "Overlord" invasion (which eventually developed into the Normandy D-Day landings). He felt this would appease Stalin enough so that the strongman's relentless, badgering demands for territory could be postponed until after the war. The American president always favored putting off difficult matters as long as possible when working on international policy.

Churchill, by contrast, wanted to launch an invasion of the Balkans, specifically to cut off a Soviet route of advance into Europe while simultaneously dealing a crippling blow to the Third Reich. Stalin, suspecting his allies of the blackest treachery as always, insisted on both advancing territorial grants to the USSR and the immediate opening of a second front to alleviate German pressure on the Soviet Union.

For most of 1943, Stalin had continued to dodge a meeting, not wishing to abandon Soviet claims on the Baltic nations and other imperial acquisitions. He sent Vyacheslav Molotov in his stead to London and Washington DC, but the ill-tempered foreign minister lacked the full authority to negotiate, which belonged to Stalin alone.

Molotov

In May 1943, Churchill had sailed to Washington, D.C., where he met with Roosevelt. The two men conferred together on the course of the war, and in the process they decided to issue a joint invitation to Stalin to meet with them in the immediate future. Churchill wrote to Stalin that "the need and advantage of a meeting are very great. I can only say I will go at any risk to any place that you and the President may agree upon. I and my advisers believe Scapa Flow, which is our main naval harbour in the North of Scotland, would be most convenient, the safest and, if secrecy be desired, probably the most secret. [...] If you could come there by air at any time in the summer you may be sure that every arrangement would be made to suit your wishes and you would have a most hearty welcome from your British and American comrades." (Ministry, 1958, 135).

Stalin responded by haranguing Churchill in a highly peremptory fashion at the Allies' "failure" to live up to their "promises" to establish a second front in Europe in 1943. The Soviet dictator went so far as to cite various Western communications on possible invasion dates, ignoring the logistical impossibility of this original, tentative timetable. He used a tone of frosty hauteur to which the peppery Prime Minister, not inclined to endure Stalin's belligerent rebukes, snapped back, "I cannot see how a great British defeat and slaughter would aid the Soviet armies. It might, however, cause the utmost ill-feeling here if it were thought it had been   incurred [...] under pressure from you. You will remember [...] that I would never authorise any cross-Channel attack which I believed would lead to only useless massacre." (Ministry, 1958, 133).

The argument between the three allies worsened over the summer. Roosevelt confessed to Churchill that he had originally planned a meeting without the prime minister, which alarmed the Englishman deeply. The Soviets withdrew their ambassadors from London and Washington, while Stalin spoke openly of working out a peace with Hitler. Only when the German attack at Kursk failed did Stalin reopen negotiations with the Western allies.

Stalin, now holding several trump cards for the meeting, finally concurred regarding the advisability of a conference. Coy as a stereotypical damsel in a medieval romance, however, the Soviet Union's overlord politely declined the invitation to Scapa Flow. He cited the need for his personal intervention at the front during the critical "German-Soviet struggle" of the summer and autumn, which prevented him from leaving his territories for even a week. This, of course, represented pure fabrication, since Stalin never went anywhere he might risk catching a stray bullet, studiously avoiding military fronts.

Once again procrastinating, Stalin accepted the idea of a summit, but suggested that the foreign ministers of the three states meet first to work out both a location and an agenda for the eventual Big Three conference. Glad to have any opportunity to talk with their thorny "ally," the Western heads of state agreed, urging a London or Casablanca meeting between the ministers. However, Stalin, once again asserting dominance, flatly declared Moscow the only acceptable site for the ministers' meeting. Months of circular argument followed, as the Western leaders proposed Cairo, the Royal Air Force base at Habbaniya in Iraq, and other sites for the conference, which Stalin constantly turned down.

Finally, the ministers' meeting occurred in Moscow, starting on October 20th, 1943. Molotov and Stalin attended, as did Sir Anthony Eden for England. Roosevelt sent Secretary of State Cordell Hull to Moscow in an effort to decisively pin down Stalin to a three-power summit in person, outside the Soviet Union's borders.

Eden

Hull

Hull, whom White House Secret Service chief Michael F. Reilly described as "the squeaky-voiced, courtly, yet adamant, hillbilly Judge from Tennessee" (Reilly, 1947, 163), carried a personal letter from Roosevelt to Stalin (translated into Russian) suggesting Basra, Baghdad, or several Turkish cities. Stalin read the paper and then blandly remarked that he could go to Fairbanks, Alaska in spring 1944.

Hull, outmaneuvered, protested that an immediate meeting represented an indispensible imperative, enabling the Big Three to agree in detail on a coordinated strategy for action in 1944. He went on to expound that meeting in Tehran created problems for Roosevelt. Though the American president refused to allow his paraplegia to cut into his mobility more than necessary, Iran was an immense distance from Washington DC. Further, with Congress soon to be in session, American law obliged Roosevelt to sign off on new legislation within 10 days, necessitating a complex system of flights to bring documents to him and return them to the US within the legally permitted window. If bad weather caused a delay, this might trigger a Constitutional crisis.

Stalin, however, remained adamant; in no case did he ever travel to a location not firmly controlled by his own troops. His murderous paranoia likely prompted him to suspect treachery from his allies as a matter of course, so he insisted on Tehran, then in Soviet (NKVD) hands, just as he later chose Yalta on the Black Sea and Soviet-occupied Potsdam in Germany for the two follow-up summits.

In the meantime, Roosevelt and Churchill decided to meet in Cairo, Egypt, regardless of whether they could persuade Stalin to meet them. The Nationalist Chinese leader, Chiang Kai-Shek also agreed to come, enabling a three-way meeting during which the Western Allies could could speak with Chiang and set up a coordinated strategy against Japan, the same way they wanted to work out a common military strategy with Stalin against Hitler.

Chiang Kai-Shek

The presence of Chiang Kai-Shek at the Cairo Conference definitely ended any possibility that Stalin would attend. The Soviet leader had no objection to supporting the Nationalist Chinese despite their enmity with Mao Tse Tung's communists. However, he studiously avoided anything which might trigger a second-front war with the Japanese. Appearing at the same conference as Chiang Kai-Shek might prove sufficient to bring the full force of the IJA rolling across the USSR's Siberian border.

The President and Prime Minister agreed to meet on November 20th in a villa around one mile from the famous Egyptian pyramids. Meanwhile, Cordell Hull frantically continued his efforts to carry out his mission, only to be stonewalled with equal stubbornness by Stalin and Molotov.

Practically on the eve of Roosevelt's departure, Stalin's agreement to meet with the president and Churchill remained in doubt. Mike Reilly, head of the Secret Service, flew ahead to North Africa to prepare security for Roosevelt's arrival. Boarding a Douglas C-54 Skymaster, the powerfully-built, utterly loyal agent flew to Cuba, then Trinidad, and then to Belem in Brazil. From Brazil, the C-54 carrying Reilly crossed the Atlantic to Dakar, then located in French West Africa (now Senegal). This flight of 2,396 miles represented over half of the aircraft's 4,000 mile range. Next, he flew to Marrakech, Morocco, arriving on the same day that Cordell Hull flew in from Moscow on his way back to the United States along the same circuitous route. The two men met in a car parked on the airfield, and Reilly learned for the first time that Stalin had finally agreed to a conference in Tehran: "When I climbed into the automobile with him his grim, yet kindly, face was wreathed in smiles. 'Stalin don't want to do much travelin' of any kind,' the Secretary told me, triumphantly, 'but I got him to go far as Teheran to meet with the President.' I told Hull that the Boss had instructed me to set up any arrangements that Hull had seen fit to conclude. 'Well, it's Teheran then,' said Hull. 'Good luck, Mike. I'll tell the President I saw you.'" (Reilly, 1947, 163).

After their brief meeting, Reilly flew on to Oran, while Hull flew in the opposite direction to Dakar. The Western Allies had finally pinned Stalin down to a definite time and place for a summit meeting between the Big Three, just a few weeks in the future. After months of trying to budge Stalin from his settled determination on "Tehran or nothing," Roosevelt and Churchill had finally yielded to the Soviet leader's obstinacy.

Chapter 2: The Big Three Travel to Tehran

With the Third Reich battling for survival but still a powerful force controlling Europe and a considerable slice of Western Russia, the Allies attempted to keep the Tehran Conference secret for the safety of those involved. Moreover, the Germans still controlled the Crimea, on the northern shores of the Black Sea, putting Iran within flying distance of their long-range aircraft. As it turned out, all of the Allied attempts to conceal the summit proved vain, but the men attempting to conceal their leaders' movements only learned this later.

Churchill and Roosevelt, with a meeting scheduled for Cairo along with Chiang Kai-Shek, started out on their travels long before Stalin left his intensively guarded Moscow headquarters. Churchill departed from England aboard the battlecruiser HMS *Renown* on November 12th. As usual on his diplomatic travels, the prime minister fell ill with a cold and fever, alarming his personal physician. Various admirals and generals accompanied him, as did his daughter Sarah, whom he described as his "aide-de-camp." Churchill recovered considerably from his illness by the time the *Renown* passed Gibraltar. He also ordered a lifeboat equipped with a machine gun so that if the Germans sank the *Renown,* he could "shoot it out" with the surfaced U-boat rather than be captured.

The *Renown*

On November 15th, Churchill reached Algiers, where he stopped off to confer with Free French General Alphonse Georges. the prime minister then sailed on to Malta, arriving on the 17th. There, General Dwight D. Eisenhower and General Sir Harold Alexander met him, at which point Churchill awarded each the North Africa Ribbon. "I had the honour of investing these two Commanders with this unique decoration. They were both taken by surprise, and seemed highly gratified when I pinned the ribbons on their coats." (Churchill, 2002, 398).

As usual, the American president faced the longest journey and the greatest difficulties in hiding his movements. Roosevelt used understated misdirection to conceal his absence from the USA. He visited the Tomb of the Unknown Soldier on November 11th, Armistice Day from World War I, along with Frank Knox and Henry Stimson, the Secretaries of the Navy and Army respectively. However, he avoided the press, likely to dodge uncomfortable questions about his whereabouts over the next few days.

The president and his party slipped out of the White House that night, driving south along U.S. Route 1 to Quantico, Virginia. There they boarded the USS *Potomac,* Roosevelt's presidential yacht, which took them to the battleship USS *Iowa,* anchored in Chesapeake Bay. Though the yacht reached the *Iowa* at 3:30 AM, the president transferred over only at 9 AM on November 12th, carried by a sturdy Secret Service man. The Secret Service effected the mostly paraplegic president's transfer unobtrusively, without any of the usual pomp attending a presidential shipboard arrival. Then, the USS *Potomac* sailed for a location where its crew hid it for two weeks, creating the subtle but unmistakable illusion Roosevelt decided to take a brief vacation somewhere in the US.

Since the *Iowa's* tanks had been pumped 80% dry to give it the necessary buoyancy to enter Chesapeake Bay, the huge battleship, skippered by Captain John McCrea, made an almost immediate refueling stop at Hampton Roads. Roosevelt concealed himself in his cabin to avoid being sighted, as did the top Army and Naval brass accompanying him: 5-star Admiral Ernest King, General George C. Marshall, Admiral William Leahy, General Henry "Hap" Arnold, and others. Nevertheless, Roosevelt dined with McCrea, and while chatting over the meal, the US Commander in Chief made a curious request: "You know, John, today is Friday. We are about to start on an important mission. Before it is over, many important decisions must be made. I am sailor enough to share a sailor's superstition that Friday is an unlucky day. Do you suppose you could delay getting underway until Saturday – this is of course without interrupting your plans too much?" (Eubank, 1985, 17).

The *Iowa*

Accordingly, the *Iowa* steamed into the Atlantic at 12:05 AM on Saturday, November 13th, though fully fueled earlier. Unbeknownst to Roosevelt, the immense Mike Reilly, with the mastiff-like fidelity he always retained, made his own secret preparations for the ocean crossing, trusting more in strong American backs than in superstitious sailing dates. Keenly aware of the possibility of U-boat attack, Reilly "found a huge Secret Service agent who could swim for hours. Every time Roosevelt boarded a heavy cruiser in the war, the swimmer was aboard. 'All you have to do,' Mike told him, 'is grab the president if anything happens to this vessel. Just grab him, jump in the water and hold his head up until help comes.'" (Bishop, 1973, 16).

Reilly's preparations almost became needed twice on the journey. Halfway across the Atlantic, one of the escorting destroyers accidentally launched a torpedo directly at the USS *Iowa*. McCrea brought the big ship around just in time for the torpedo to rush past parallel to the hull rather than striking it. The naval officers calculated its trajectory and estimated that without the evasive turn, it would have struck the hull immediately below Roosevelt's cabin, possibly killing him outright.

Worse, alarming signs appeared that the Germans knew of Roosevelt's sailing, his destination, and even his approximate timetable. With the *Iowa* just two days out from the Straits of Gibraltar, the Germans suddenly deployed their new G7es T5 Zaunkonig, or Wren, an acoustic torpedo with great vigor against ships traversing the Straits. Rather than running in a straight line, the G7es torpedo homed in on the target via a passive acoustic sensor, which activated an electropneumatic rudder to steer the ordnance to its prey.

The Americans in North Africa, including Mike Reilly, radioed the USS *Iowa* with an urgent warning to steer clear of the Straits, and the presidential convoy accordingly turned towards the alternate port of Dakar. However, just one hour later, US Intelligence in North Africa learned of large shoals of U-boats lurking off Dakar. Once again informed of the situation, the *Iowa* turned towards the Straits afresh while the Allies stepped up anti-submarine measures there. Aircraft sank one U-boat and the *Iowa* passed through safely at night, docking in Oran on November 20th.

Roosevelt, Churchill, and Chiang Kai-Shek held the conference at Cairo as planned, after which the Anglo-American leaders prepared to fly on to Tehran on the morning of November 27th. After a delay due to fog, the aircraft set out, flying low due to the effects of altitude on Roosevelt's sinuses and general health. Roosevelt recorded his impressions of the Middle Eastern landscape: "On Saturday we passed over Bethlehem and Jerusalem – everything very bare looking – and I don't want Palestine as my homeland. Then hundreds of miles of Arabian desert, then a green ribbon and Baghdad and the Tigris, with another green ribbon, the Euphrates – bare mountains and we followed the highway over which so much lend lease goes to Russia. Then a vast plain or saucer with Tehran and its snow peaks to the north." (Eubank, 1985, 175-176).

Stalin preferred to travel by rail whenever he could, considering it much safer than flying, which terrified him. He probably deemed that internal enemies could more easily contrive a fatal accident involving an aircraft (where any system failure or explosion above a low altitude spelled certain death for the occupants) than a train (larger and therefore less subject to instant destruction, and on the ground, where escape remained possible). To reach Tehran, however, the Soviet dictator necessarily took to the air. He traveled by train as far as Baku, in Azerbaijan, on the shores of the Caspian Sea. A rumor or legend exists that Stalin visited the scenes of his first youthful bank robberies in Baku. Regardless of possible sentimentality, he boarded an aircraft at Baku airfield.

Even at this moment, however, he remained as wily and paranoid as ever. The Soviets prepared two aircraft for the trip to Tehran, carrying assorted generals, Stalin, his Foreign Secretary Vyacheslav Molotov, and Lavrenty Beria, the sinister, bespectacled USSR Minister of Internal Affairs. Head of the NKVD secret police, Beria also engaged in numerous rapes and probable serial killings of young women, and he has even been accused of murdering Stalin in 1953 to secure his own brief, bloodily terminated ascendancy.

According to plan, Stalin would fly on one airplane piloted by Marshal of Aviation Alexander Golovanov, while Beria and his son Sergo Beria would fly on the other aircraft, piloted by Colonel V.G. Grachev. However, when Stalin stepped out of his car on the Baku airfield at 8 AM, he took a few steps towards Golovanov's transport, then abruptly halted, announcing that the Berias would fly with Golovanov and he would board Grachev's plane – undoubtedly a precaution against assassination. Golovanov, standing as if upset at the seeming snub, drew the dictator's attention. Stalin, with a mix of kindliness and mockery, stated to the embarrassed Marshal of Aviation, "Don't take it badly, but it seems to me that colonels have more experience than generals where flying is concerned." (Beria, 2001, 92).

Beria

Most of the men in Stalin's entourage learned for the first time that they would fly to Tehran as the American-built Douglas C-54 Skymaster transports, acquired through Lend-Lease, rumbled down the Baku airstrip. The Soviet leader used secrecy in addition to brute force to ensure his safety, and the "Man of Steel" also arranged for security along the way or in Tehran. 36 Soviet fighter aircraft accompanied the C-54s, arranged in four squadrons of 9 aircraft apiece, one leading, one above the transports, and one flanking the two Skymasters to either side. The destination, Tehran, already swarmed with 3,000 NKVD soldiers in preparation for the Soviet premier's arrival.

Due to Lend-Lease and the recent ousting of Nazi agents and forces from Iran, the country also swarmed with British and Americans. The US Army encamped some 30,000 troops within a stone's throw of Tehran, while the British also maintained soldiers in the country to watch both their interests and the rail lines. Additionally, US General Norman Schwarzkopf, Sr. had organized a formidable local "gendarmerie."

Chapter 3: The Beginning of the Conference

The Big Three at Tehran

The Eureka Conference, as Winston Churchill (who always delighted in choosing codenames) dubbed it, took place in one of the remotest areas of the early 1940s. Roosevelt summarized the city in a single word – "dirty" – while a German, Bernhardt Schulze-Holthus, managed to wax rhapsodic over Tehran's "old town with a network of narrow alleys and the covered-in passages of the bazaars in whose magical twilight the riches of the land seemed to be piled, as in Aladdin's cave – barbaric carpets, miniature paintings, wonderful tarsia work of precious woods and the sparkling splendor of the silversmith's craft. The life in this old town [...] flows faster than in the smart streets of the government quarter." (Yelle, 2015, 35).

The British and Soviet legations stood near the city center, flanking a narrow street, with a high defensible wall around them. The American legation, by contrast, stood at the fringes of the city some four miles distant from the other two. The legations represented most of the few buildings with running water in the city, and among the only ones free of infestation of typhus lice infestations. Both Churchill and Stalin issued warm invitations to the American president to stay at their legation instead, but Roosevelt initially declined, preferring, as he said, to retain more independence.

Roosevelt's aircraft set down at Gale Morghe airfield at 3 PM, the same one where the Americans delivered Lend-Lease aircraft which Soviet pilots then flew to Russia. He drove directly to the American legation with a powerful escort of armed soldiers in Jeeps and M3A1 armored cars. Both on the way and on arrival the Soviets repeated their cordial offers to house Roosevelt at the Russian legation, meeting polite refusals each time.

Churchill, landing separately, found himself in an alarmingly exposed open car driving slowly along a carefully marked route. He noted that the widely-spaced cavalrymen along the way, though intended as a guard of honor, instead served as signposts above the crowd showing exactly where an assassin could find him. Though he arrived safely at his national legation, the prime minister later described the scene with his usual mix of eloquent sarcasm, touched with some humor: "As we reached the turning which led to the Legation there was a traffic block, and we remained for three or four minutes stationary amid the crowded throng of gaping Persians. If it had been planned out beforehand to run the greatest risks, and have neither the security of quiet surprise arrival nor an effective escort, the problem could not have been solved more perfectly. However, nothing happened. I grinned at the crowd, and on the whole they grinned at me." (Churchill, 2002, 418).

Roosevelt issued an invitation to Stalin to come share dinner with him, but the Soviet strongman declined. Another invitation to Churchill met with a similar refusal – the prime minister had managed to catch yet another of his traveling colds and had taken to his bed with a novel and a bottle of whiskey. FDR found himself left to the company of his fellow countrymen during the first evening in Tehran, though Averell Harriman managed to secure Stalin's agreement to hold the first plenary session at the American legation the following day.

Harriman

With a perfect sense of dramatic timing, messengers arrived at the American legation at midnight, having hastened through the darkened streets at the bidding of Molotov. These Soviets brought a report of German SD Sonderlehrgang paratroopers or commandos loose in the city, looking to kill Roosevelt, Stalin, and Churchill alike. The Soviets primed Mike Reilly with such stories from his earliest arrival to make security arrangements for Roosevelt and the American officials and military men accompanying him. General Dmitry Arkadiev of the NKVD transportation division had gotten friendly with Reilly, and informed him of the capture of six Nazi radio operators in Tehran. This story soon blossomed into dozens of paratrooper assassins dropped by night-flying aircraft launched from the German-held Crimea.

The existence of the German paratroopers remains a matter of historical contention. No non-Soviet source exists for this plan, called "Operation Long Jump," or *Unternehmen Weitsprung* in German. Though the NKVD men speaking with Reilly and the other Americans spoke of the British capturing some of the German assassins, no known British account refers firsthand to such an event. The names of the two leading assassins, SS Sturmbannfuhrer Hans Ulrich von Ortel and the "criminal" Abwehr agent Lothar Schoellhorn appear nowhere else in history, including the muster rolls of the organizations to which they purportedly belonged.

The famous German commando Otto Skorzeny dismissed the entire Operation Long Jump plot as a Soviet fabrication in his postwar memoirs: "In reality Operation Weitsprung existed only in the imaginations of a few truth-loving scribes or for the 'fellow comrades' of Bolshevism. Stalin succeeded in isolating Churchill at Tehran, and the British prime minister was forced to accept the proposals of his two interlocutors." (Skorzeny, 1995, 207).

Skorzeny noted that the Germans knew of the Eureka summit and briefly entertained the idea of killing the three Allied leaders there. However, the infeasibility of the project caused Skorzeny to speak out against it to Hitler. He pointed out that large numbers of superbly trained men would be needed, along with equipment, vehicles, and aircraft the Germans could not transport to Iran. After Skorzeny listed all of the objections, pointing out the tiny chance of success when tens of thousands of Allied troops and security swarmed through Tehran, while the Germans had no information whatsoever about security arrangements, the Fuhrer concurred.

According to the famous commando, Operation Long Jump never even reached the planning stages. He speculated that the NKVD learned of the idea through the "Red Orchestra" in Germany and developed it for their own purposes. The stories, however, appeared less far-fetched to Reilly and the other men charged with Roosevelt's security. With a necessarily limited view of the strategic situation and tactical difficulties, the Secret Service and American forces simply heard that a threat to their leader existed in a remote, hostile, and unpredictable country.

Told of the alleged German assassins the following morning, Roosevelt decided to relocate to the Soviet embassy. His men had already inspected the quarters repeatedly and found them sufficiently commodious. Some of the Americans, such as the presidential interpreter and Russian expert Charles E. Bohlen, suspected the threat might prove bogus, but the president remained disinclined to listen.

That morning, US military police and soldiers lined the four mile route from the American to the Soviet legations. A convoy of Jeeps and armored cars started out along this path, with the presidential car sandwiched in the middle. This imposing display rolled slowly through the streets, while crowds of locals formed behind the cordon of American military personnel to watch the pomp and circumstance of the President on the move.

The convoy, in fact, represented a spectacular decoy meant to draw away any German or Iranian assassins. Reilly carried Roosevelt unobtrusively out to a second car in an alley near the American legation. Accompanied by just one Jeep, the car sped through Tehran's back streets, unnoticed by any ill-wishers along the route. Roosevelt arrived through a side entrance of the Soviet legation, in excellent spirits after his adventure.

Regardless of whether German commandos actually operated in Iran during the summit, the change of quarters caused by reports of them placed Roosevelt exactly where the Soviets wanted him. The NKVD festooned the quarters provided to the Americans at the legation with concealed microphones, enabling the Soviets to listen clearly to every talk occurring there, regardless of the room or hallway in question.

Stalin placed responsibility for eavesdropping on the Americans in the hands of the young Sergo Beria. The dictator gave his instructions to Sergo thus: "I want to entrust you with a mission that is delicate and morally reprehensible. You are going to listen to the conversations Roosevelt will have with Churchill, with the other British, and with his own circle. I must know everything in detail, be aware of all the shades of meaning. I am asking you for all that because it is now that the question of the second front will be settled. I know that Churchill is against it. It is important that the Americans support us in this matter." (Beria, 2001, 93).

Beria's description of the process involved in spying on the foreigners sheds interesting light on both NKVD methods and Stalin's thought processes, which the dictator often concealed. Sergo rose early to prepare the translated transcripts of the Western Allies' conversations from the previous evening, with the help of his staff. At 8 AM Stalin arrived to read over the transcripts with the younger Beria. The Soviet dictator read the papers, quizzing Sergo on the details of tone used by the participants in the bugged conversations. He wanted to know the emotional state of each speaker just as much as he desired the actual content of their discussions. Stalin repeatedly expressed complete astonishment over the frankness the Americans used while speaking, describing their honesty as "bizarre."

Moreover, Sergo and Lavrenty Beria discussed the information gained in private, forming their own opinions of their current allies and possible future enemies. The father and son grew convinced that Roosevelt's chief obsession lay in dismantling the British Empire, and his interests in World War II consisted of ridding himself of the European theater as quickly as possible so as to concentrate on the war with Japan, and to limit American casualties.

While some of Roosevelt's aides warned him that the Soviets probably prepared the rooms with listening devices, the president dismissed these fears. William Bullitt, a former ambassador to the Soviet Union who described Stalin vividly as "a Caucasian bandit whose only thought when he got something for nothing was that the other fellow was an ass," claimed that Roosevelt told him, "Bill, I don't dispute your facts; they are accurate. I don't dispute the logic of your reasoning. I just have a hunch that Stalin is not that kind of man. [...] I think if I give him everything I possibly can and ask for nothing in return, noblesse oblige, he won't try to annex anything and will work with me for a world of democracy and peace." (Bullitt, 1948, 94).

Bullitt later blasted Roosevelt's "ostrich infantilism" and dubbed him "Alice in Blunderland," but Roosevelt remained convinced that Stalin could be won over to peace, democracy, and even conversion to Christianity from Soviet atheism if he gave the dictator everything he wanted and concealed nothing from him. Such a mindset might come across (thorough eavesdropping) as a major benefit, helping win the Soviets' trust and showing them the Americans had no ulterior motives. The evidence, however, suggests nothing could win Stalin's trust or change the "Red Czar's" purposes, motivated by a cold, unswerving, deeply aggressive will to power.

Stalin arrived almost immediately at Roosevelt's quarters after the American president's arrival.

Charles Bohlen, who would serve as Roosevelt's interpreter, saw his chief at close quarters for the first time and noticed that he seemed at the peak of his powers: "Except for one minor incident, he seemed to be in excellent health, never showing any signs of fatigue, and holding his magnificent leonine head high. He clearly was the dominating figure at the conference. I found him pleasant and considerate and his personal touch made our association agreeable." (Bohlen, 1973, 147).

Bohlen

Bohlen provided translation during the historic first meeting of the American and Soviet leaders, while V. Pavlov accomplished the same task on the Soviet side. The two powerful men greeted each other cordially and after a brief exchange of pleasantries began chatting informally about the military situation and the topics for the conference. Stalin told Roosevelt that the situation along the Eastern Front remained difficult and the Red Army could probably only mount offensives in the Ukraine in the immediate future. Roosevelt responded that he wanted to take military actions sufficient to draw 30-40 divisions away from the Eastern Front, which pleased the Soviet premier. When Stalin asked if they should set up a precise schedule for the summit, Roosevelt responded, "I don't think we should rigidly define the range of topics. We might simply have a general exchange of views about the situation and the prospects. I would also be interested to hear from you about the position on the Soviet-German front." (Eubank,

1985, 245).

The two leaders continued talking, Roosevelt sketching out his ideas about the conduct of the war and Stalin mostly agreeing. The president noted that supporting two million American soldiers in Europe required vast amounts of new shipping construction and that these vessels might find their way to the USSR following the war. He also gave Stalin a few pertinent details of his meeting with Chiang Kai-Shek.

Stalin next queried Roosevelt about the French and Charles de Gaulle. The two men agreed that due to "collaborating" with Germany, the French should be stripped of their colonial possessions, and that no Frenchman over 40 years old should be allowed to hold public office again in their lifetimes, in addition to any younger Frenchmen who worked for the Vichy government. Stalin's remarkable hostility to France and de Gaulle roused Bohlen's suspicion that the generalissimo disliked the idea of a strong French nation which might help check Soviet ambitions in the West, though he kept this to himself.

Roosevelt then jumped to the question of India, saying that he wanted it "reformed from the bottom up," like Soviet Russia. Even Stalin balked it this, remarking that such a reform would actually constitute a violent revolution. Roosevelt also noted that they should avoid mentioning India to Churchill. The tenor of the conversation clearly envisioned Roosevelt and Stalin deciding the fate of the world together, leaving Churchill out of the process as much as possible. Whether this represented Roosevelt's position or simply diplomatic flattery of Stalin remained unclear to the observers and interpreters.

If the two chiefs reached a temporary measure of understanding, however, their bodyguards did not. Mike Reilly reported, with a hint of dry humor, "[Stalin] and the Boss got down to the baffling business of carrying on a conversation through interpreters while the NKVD boys and I exchanged long, rude stares. While the two biggest men in the world talked of the destinies of millions, their personal bodyguards played a very silly game of trying to stare each other down. It resulted in a draw." (Reilly, 1947, 180).

With this prelude out of the way, Roosevelt and Stalin left with their interpreters and guards to meet with Churchill and commence the first Plenary Session of a conference destined to last just four days but settle important questions about the opening of a second front in Europe – while raising future issues concerning the postwar world.

Chapter 4: November 28

Representatives from each of the major Allied powers attended the first plenary session of the Eureka Summit. The conference room, in the American section of the Soviet legation for Roosevelt's convenience, featured posh décor, including tapestries on the walls and elegant curtains on the windows. Outside, what Charles Bohlen described as a "beautiful Iranian Sunday afternoon, gold and blue, mild and sunny" welcomed Churchill and his party as they strolled over from the British legation.

The delegates gathered around a large round table, chosen, like that of the legendary King Arthur, to avoid giving any of the three leaders a symbolic advantage over the others. Covered in green baize cloth, this table served for all four of the plenary sessions comprising the Tehran Conference.

The men assembled for the first plenary session at 4 PM presented a rather martial look. With the war at its height, more generals, marshals, and admirals sat at the table than civilian statesmen. Hard-eyed, watchful NKVD soldiers stood against the chamber's walls, while the Secret Service and US and British military police guarded outside.

Roosevelt, Charles Bohlen, Averell Harriman, Admirals William Leahy and Ernest King, Major General John Russell Deane, a USN captain, and Harry Hopkins (then slowly dying of stomach cancer, but curiously revived by wartime responsibilities) represented the United States. US Army Chief of Staff General George C. Marshall and USAF General Henry "Hap" Arnold failed to attend due to scheduling confusion. The British delegation included Churchill, Foreign Secretary Sir Anthony Eden, Field Marshal Sir John Dill, Chief of the Imperial General Staff General Alan Brooke, Admiral Andrew Cunningham, RAF Marshal Charles Portal, Lieutenant General Hastings "Pug" Ismay, and Major Arthur H. Birse as the interpreter, while Stalin joined Molotov, the interpreter Pavlov, Marshal Kliment Voroshilov, and another interpreter, Valentin Berezhkov.

Bohlen noted the surprisingly relaxed atmosphere. Each party's interpreter translated their remarks in order to minimize the chance of a misunderstanding due to poorly translated idiomatic phrases or other errors. Stalin appeared on his best behavior. Dealing with Russians, the Soviet dictator adopted a barking, peremptory tone, impatient, angry, and overbearing, in order to establish his dominance. However, speaking to the foreigners, he talked quietly, used qualifying phrases such as "in my opinion," and smiled frequently. The Americans noted he never smiled at Russians.

Both Roosevelt and Stalin spoke in relatively brief sections, enabling their interpreters to translate without undue strain and allowing the stenographers to record their words. Churchill, however, often made long-winded speeches that left Arthur Birse struggling to catch up. Bohlen claimed the prime minister never spoke for less than 5-6 minutes continuously. Nevertheless, Birse remained enthralled by Churchill's eloquence, as his memoirs describe, providing a lively portrait of "Winnie" in action: "His remarks were prefaced by a kind of suppressed murmur, as if he were trying out the richness of his words while on their way from brain to tongue, as if he were repeating them to himself, testing them, discarding the inappropriate, and choosing precisely the right expression. I could almost hear them traveling from the depths of his being to burst into life." (Birse, 1967, 100).

Roosevelt spoke first, welcoming the other two heads of state as his elders. He expressed the hope they could work together as a family, with complete frankness, to cooperate in winning the war and create a partnership between their countries which would last for generations. Churchill added that the Big Three wielded the greatest power in history, and they should use it wisely to shorten the war, while Stalin welcomed the other two men and their entourages, adding sentiments similar to Roosevelt's.

Roosevelt opened the plenary session by describing America's commitment to the Pacific theater, including the deployment of over a million men. He noted that the US strategy showed strong signs of success, maintaining China in the war (thus tying up huge numbers of Japanese soldiers) and sinking more tonnage of Japanese ships than the enemy could manufacture. He described the start of the island-hopping campaign and plans for a a major offensive into Burma under Louis Mountbatten.

He then turned to the question of Europe, noting that shipping represented the biggest issue, but that he intended to send at least 1 million men ashore in northern France by May 1st, 1944 in the invasion codenamed Operation Overlord. He noted that the English Channel represented a "disagreeable" body of water, at which Churchill interjected that the Channel's unpleasantness also provided benefits, referring to the lack of a German invasion early in the war.

Roosevelt noted that the possibility of a Mediterranean diversion – an attack in the French Riviera, more action in Italy, an invasion of the Balkans – presented difficulties due to the shortage of landing craft. He addressed the Soviets directly at this point: "[C]ertain contemplated operations in the Mediterranean might result in a delay in Overlord for one month or two or three. Therefore, I pray in this military Conference to have the benefit of the opinion of the two Soviet Marshals and that they will inform us how in their opinion we can be of most help to the USSR." (Franklin, 1961, 890).

Roosevelt completed his presentation by saying that the whole purpose of the Western attack centered on drawing as many Wehrmacht divisions as possible away from the Eastern Front.

Churchill spoke next, at this point largely confirming the president's words, though he put more emphasis on Mediterranean operations.

Stalin responded to Roosevelt's statement in a smooth, cogent manner. He congratulated the United States on its military successes in the Pacific, but noted with apparent regret that the Red Army could not yet help in that theater. He noted how the front with the Germans demanded all available resources, telling everyone, "We [...] are unable to launch any operations against Japan at this time. Our forces now in the East are more or less satisfactory for defense. However, they must be increased about three-fold for purposes of offensive operations. This condition will not take place until Germany has been forced to capitulate. Then by our common front we shall win." (Franklin, 1961, 891).

With Roosevelt's and Churchill's permission, Stalin provided a detailed description of the strategic situation on the Eastern Front. He stated that the Third Reich mustered 260 divisions there, 210 of them German and 50 drawn from other countries, with an additional half-dozen on the way. The Red Army outnumbered these by 70 divisions, fielding 330 divisions in all, enabling the start of offensive operations.

The Soviet strongman went on to offer his opinion on the Western Allies' operations. He said that since the Allies now had enough ground in Italy to ensure large Lend-Lease shipments through the Mediterranean, they ought to avoid committing more troops to Italy, which would provide no additional benefit. He said that an invasion of northwestern or southern France presented the best strategic option, but reminded his listeners that "it must be expected that the Germans will fight like devils to prevent such an attack."

After Stalin finished, Churchill held the floor. He emphasized again the Western Allies' firm intention to invade France with at least a million men regardless of operations elsewhere. Then he went on for a considerable time, arguing for an invasion of southern France, stronger efforts in Italy, and an attempt to bring Turkey into the war. He dwelt on Turkey for some time, noting how it would provide superb forward airbases for both the Anglo-American and Soviet air forces to launch attacks deep into German territory. The addition of Turkey to the Allied cause might also, he averred, prompt countries such as Greece to rise in rebellion against the German occupiers and oust them from their territory.

Stalin, however, dismissed the notion that the Turks would assist the Allies, at least not until it became evident the Germans teetered on the brink of destruction. He also argued against breaking up the available Allied forces in the West into multiple smaller fronts, instead suggesting one major offensive – in effect, what the Wehrmacht called a "*Schwerpunkt*" – "focal point," literally "hard point" – in northwestern France. He proposed that the Allies remove 10 divisions from Italy and use them to invade southern France as a second pincer, thus avoiding the weakening of the main strength flowing across the Channel. The Soviet generalissimo here cited Red Army experience that an offensive at one point usually failed regardless of its strength, but that a secondary offensive launched simultaneously usually produced excellent results.

Churchill found Stalin's comments "interesting" but insisted on the necessity to take Rome, both to acquire air bases to support the southern French landings and to protect Anglo-American military reputation. He then returned to the subject of Turkey, leading to a rather pithy exchange between the two men: "When I said that Turkey would be mad if she declined Russia's invitation to come in on the winning side, and at the same time lost the sympathy of Great Britain, Stalin rejoined that a number of people preferred to be mad, and all neutrals regarded those who were waging war as fools to fight when they might be doing nothing." (Churchill, 2002, 436).

Roosevelt intervened at this point to say that he would try to pressure Turkey into entering the war on the Allied side. He issued the caveat, however, that he thought the Turks would want so much support in exchange that it would endanger the success of Operation Overlord.

At this point, the first plenary session wound down. The Big Three agreed to convene again at 4 PM the next day, and that their military chiefs would hold a separate preparatory session at 10:30 AM.

As at the later Yalta and Potsdam conferences, the Big Three held a dinner party after each plenary session. The first night's supper occurred at Roosevelt's quarters. The Filipino cooks brought on the USS *Iowa* prepared a meal of steak and baked potatoes, while the president himself readied the cocktails, as Bohlen described: "Roosevelt mixed the pre-dinner cocktails himself, a ceremony he enjoyed. Roosevelt was proud of his drinks, which were unlike anything I have ever tasted. He put a large quantity of vermouth, both sweet and dry, into a pitcher of ice, added a smaller amount of gin, stirred the concoction rapidly, and poured it out. Stalin accepted the glass and drank but made no comment." (Bohlen, 1973), 143).

FDR's skills as bartender might perhaps have fallen somewhat below his own estimation, because he soon abruptly turned "green" in Bohlen's words, while a profuse sweat appeared on his face. This terrified his fellow Americans and alarmed the foreigners, until Roosevelt's personal physician declared it nothing worse than indigestion.

Roosevelt retired for the night, but the other men continued eating and talking. Churchill, at this juncture, made a casual suggestion which haunted him later. Using matchsticks, he indicated his idea for carving out a piece of Germany and giving it to Poland after the war, while leaving the portion of the country seized during the Nazi-Soviet alliance in Stalin's hands.

Stalin also returned repeatedly to several topics. He remained eager to acquire the Baltic nations, insisted that the French should be punished for the German occupation through loss of their empire and perhaps other means, and wanted harsh terms imposed to Germany, though he still opposed unconditional surrender.

Chapter 5: November 29

The Eureka Summit continued on November 29th with the meeting of military chiefs at 10:30 AM. Roosevelt had recovered fully from the previous night's problems by morning, making him capable of participating fully in the day's negotiations, but Churchill felt deep alarm at the course of the conference up to this point. Roosevelt chose to talk privately with Stalin on the first day, and not with him, and he had then taken the side of the Soviet dictator on most of the important matters discussed in the first plenary session. With characteristic eloquence, he described the menacing situation in which he found himself and his nation: "There I sat with the great Russian bear on one side of me, with paws outstretched, and on the other side the great American buffalo, and between the two sat the poor little English donkey, who was the only one […] who knew the right way home." (Eubank, 1985, 280).

Nothing that happened on the second day of the summit altered Churchill's assessment. In fact, the events deepened his alarm. Many of the American delegation shared his fears, albeit in a less Anglocentric fashion; but though his advisers believed he put too much trust in the Soviet dictator who occasionally threatened throughout the war to make peace with Hitler if his allies failed to accede to his demands, Roosevelt remained determined to win the generalissimo's "friendship."

Making up for the accidental absence of General George C. Marshall at the first day's session, military representatives of the three major allies met to continue the discussion of Overlord in more practical terms than the politicians could perhaps offer. The Soviets sent just one representative, Marshal Kliment Voroshilov, whose small eyes, wide face, and long upper lip gave him the look of a stereotypical Soviet functionary from Western propaganda. General Sir Alan Brooke and RAF Marshal Charles Portal represented the British military, while Admiral Leahy and General Marshall spoke for the US Navy and Army respectively.

Voroshilov

Marshall

Brooke

General Brooke opened the meeting with English suavity, expressing his pleasure at being able to meet his foreign military counterparts. He then launched into an immediate description of how Overlord would perform the vital function of drawing German divisions away from the Eastern Front. He then went on to point out that around 6 months would elapse prior to Overlord's launch, and he proposed that in the meantime, reinforced Mediterranean operations would provide a much-needed distraction that bled off Wehrmacht strength from more vital fronts.

Brooke described how the Italian front currently pinned down approximately 23 German divisions. In order to keep up the pressure, the British wanted to use landing craft to outflank the Germans in Italy via amphibious landings, even if this meant not using the craft as part of Overlord.

General Brooke also talked about Yugoslavia, where the partisans of Marshal Josip Broz Tito kept up a fight that prompted 21 German divisions and 8 Bulgarian divisions to remain in the Balkans and Eastern Europe to maintain the peace. The British wanted to supply Tito with more weaponry, though Voroshilov interposed at this point to say he believed the British overestimated the number of Wehrmacht divisions in the region.

Tito

Brooke pressed on, elaborating on the advantages of bringing Turkey into the war, and the number of men who would be assigned to air defense if the Allies opened major airfields in Anatolia. He then said that the British agreed with Stalin's idea for a double invasion, and thought the southern French landing should occur simultaneous with Overlord, rather than earlier, to ensure the Germans did not crush it.

General Marshall then offered a rundown of the American military situation. He stated the US had 50 divisions ready in its country and only the lack of transport currently prevented their deployment. In particular, the US needed to build additional LSTs (Landing Ship – Tank) to bring its mechanized power ashore, permitting the full unleashing of America's combined arms military forces. The conference minutes note, "General Marshall said that one reason for favoring Overlord from the start is that it is the shortest oversea transport route. After the initial success, transports will be sent directly from the United States to the French ports because there are about sixty divisions in the United States to be put into Overlord." (Franklin, 1961, 960).

Air Marshal Charles Portal then took the floor, describing the use of Spitfires, P-38 Lightnings, and P-51 Mustangs to support the Overlord landings. He then delineated the massive scale of strategic bombing directed against Germany.

Finally, Admiral Leahy intervened to ask Voroshilov to offer his opinions. Taking his cue from Stalin, Voroshilov went on the offensive, putting his allies on the defensive with a series of piercing questions. He naturally echoed his generalissimo's single-minded, obsessive focus on Overlord, while dismissing the Mediterranean theater as an unimportant sideshow.

He first asked, sensing a difference of opinion he could exploit, if the British believed Overlord as important as the Americans clearly did. Brooke, caught unawares, said that the invasion of northwestern France represented a very important part of the strategy, but gave the impression that the British remained less enthusiastic about it than their US allies.

Having gained the initiative and the dominating position, Voroshilov hammered home that Stalin *insisted* on the agreed-upon May 1st date for Overlord (D-Day). He assured the Americans they would win a great victory, and offered his opinion, based on major Soviet river crossings, that air superiority and overwhelming concentration of force would produce the desired results. To this, Marshall responded, "The difference between a river crossing, however wide [...] and a landing from the ocean is that the failure of a river crossing is a reverse while the failure of a landing operation from the sea is a catastrophe, because a failure in the latter case means the almost utter destruction of the landing craft and personnel involved." (Cray, 2000, 431-432).

Voroshilov shot back, "If you think about it, you will do it." He went on to ask details about the American landing craft types, their speed of production, and other pertinent questions. He then emphasized over and over, with dogged repetitiveness, that the Western Allies should put almost all their forces into Overlord. The southern French attack, he stated, should be much smaller and purely diversionary.

The Soviet marshal then offered his opinion on how to make the D-Day landings successful. He suggested opening with a massive artillery and bombing attack against the defenders at the landing point. Light forces and commandos should follow up, occupying key positions, after which the main forces could come ashore.

By this time, the military men had used up all the time allotted to their meeting. Since all of them felt that more needed to be discussed, they agreed to meet again the following day, November 30th, at 10:30 AM, to resume their dialogue.

Prime Minister Winston Churchill, trying to patch up the situation between the Americans and English, sent a lunch invitation to Roosevelt on the 28th, but the president turned him down. Instead, he opted to share a meal with Stalin, at which the two leaders discussed important matters in the absence of their British colleague. Roosevelt, after the expected greetings, opened the private conversation by handing the Soviet leader a paper describing Marshal Tito's partisan operations by an American officer who had spent some time with the Yugoslavian leader. He also handed the generalissimo a document proposing the use of Soviet airfields for USAF bombers, enabling shuttle-bombing between the bases in England Russia. Shuttle-bombing involved flying an aircraft straight through across the target to a base on the far side, where crews rearmed it for a second bombing attack on its way back to its home base. Stalin accepted both documents with thanks, stating he would read and consider them.

Roosevelt then described to Stalin his idea for the United Nations. He suggested that the active arm of the organization be "the Four Policemen": the USA, USSR, UK, and China. Stalin agreed with much of the framework in principle, but stated that China likely would not possess the strength after the war to assist. He also noted that the "Policemen" must hold a series of strong points, putting Germany and Japan at too much of a disadvantage to attempt military adventurism again. Roosevelt, eager to please his "friend," agreed with everything Stalin said.

As the three delegates of the major Allies and their staffs gathered immediately before the summit's next plenary session, Churchill interrupted the proceedings with an unexpected gesture. He approached Stalin with an award from his monarch: "I presented, by the King's command, the Sword of Honour which His Majesty had had specially designed and wrought to commemorate the glorious defence of Stalingrad. [...] When, after a few sentences of explanation, I handed the splendid weapon to Marshal Stalin, he raised it in a most impressive gesture to his lips and kissed the blade. He then handed it to Voroshilov, who dropped it." (Churchill, 2002, 442).

The British presentation of the Sword of Stalingrad to Stalin

Despite Voroshilov's fumbling, the Soviet officers quickly retrieved the ceremonial blade and organized a guard of honor for it. This honor guard carried the sword solemnly from the room after showing it to President Roosevelt, who expressed curiosity about the weapon. Churchill claimed that FDR at least showed signs of being moved by the ritual.

A picture of Roosevelt looking at the sword

The second plenary session opened with General Sir Alan Brooke, Marshal Kliment Voroshilov, and General George C. Marshall providing their individual summaries of the morning's military committee meeting. The three men described the current military situation relating to Operation Overlord, including the manufacture of landing ships and Marshall's observation that northwestern France lay closest to American ports.

When they described the outcome of their meeting, however, it quickly appeared that they had not come to any decision or recommendation about the operation. Their disputes, in fact, mirrored those of their heads of state. The Americans favored the May 1st date mentioned at Quebec and a heavy emphasis on the northern invasion. The British wanted to keep the date uncertain and preferred heavier operations in the Mediterranean, even if this meant delaying

Overlord. The Soviets thought the British wanted to avoid the landings entirely and forcefully urged a binding declaration of an invasion date. The three military men then reported they had postponed further discussion until the following morning.

The talk of the Big Three at the meeting followed much the same circular pattern as the wrangling of their military subordinates. Churchill stubbornly defended the British fixation on the Mediterranean theater and his wish to bring Turkey into the war. He spoke at immense length, a habit with him regardless of circumstances.

Roosevelt supported the idea of a May landing, while Stalin returned to the topic with the same relentless, fixed determination that he showed the previous day, and which Voroshilov exhibited in the morning meeting. Clearly, the Soviet dictator disbelieved the Western Allies' claims of launching a cross-Channel invasion and wanted to badger them into actually carrying it out.

Charles Bohlen noted this almost monomaniacal insistence, along with interesting details of Stalin's negotiating style: "Stalin pressed for a decision to launch Overlord in May, saying, 'I don't care if it is the 1st, 15th, or 20th, but a definite date is important.' [...] Stalin's words came out in an almost matter-of-fact tone. [...] Stalin would occasionally read from a prepared document, but most of the time he spoke extemporaneously, doodling wolf heads on a pad with a red pencil, and pausing considerably so that the interpreter could translate." (Bohlen, 1973, 145).

Stalin declared that Turkey would not enter the war, and that in any case, Overlord must be the focus of all the Western efforts. He further opined that sending weapons, money, and equipment to Eastern European partisans represented a worthwhile effort, but that this should not distract from developing and executing Overlord. He approved of the notion of a landing in south France, but it must be subordinated to Overlord.

Besides his endless insistence on Overlord first, last, and always, the generalissimo urged the Western Allies to choose a supreme commander for the operation. He opined that unless they picked one man to head and coordinate the D-Day landings, the operation would never actually occur. Churchill and Roosevelt replied that they believed an American general ought to be chosen, and that they would make the selection within two weeks.

Still, this plan failed to satisfy Stalin. While he stated he had no input on exactly who the Western Allies should choose, the USSR's supreme leader urged the other two men to pick an overall commander for Overlord immediately, during the Tehran summit. Failing that, they should pick him within one week and no longer.

After hours of circular arguing, Churchill suggested that the Big Three await the recommendations of the next military committee meeting. Stalin scoffed at this: "What can such a committee do? [...] We Chiefs of State have more power and more authority than a committee.

General Brooke cannot force our opinions and there are many questions which can be decided only by us." (Franklin, 1961, 945).

While Churchill and Brooke felt discomfited by this entire exchange, Roosevelt emerged from the session in an excellent mood. To his son Elliot, FDR later commented that Churchill's purpose consisted of keeping Stalin out of Europe. He spoke of Stalin in glowing terms: "He gets things done, that man. He really keeps his eye on the ball he's aiming at." (Cray, 2000, 434). In all, Roosevelt seemed to view him as a solid negotiating partner helping to curb the "unreasonable" Churchill.

The meeting ended with no unanimous decision about the Overlord landings or possible Mediterranean operations. The Big Three agreed to meet again for dinner in an hour, this time hosted by the Soviets. The third plenary session, they decided, would occur at 4 PM the following day.

The second night's dinner witnessed many convivial toasts at its beginning. However, under a cloak of charm, Stalin took the opportunity to harass Churchill steadily throughout the evening. The British prime minister shrugged off most of the statements directed at him. No stranger to verbal wordplay himself, he even countered some of Stalin's seemingly friendly, but extremely persistent, sallies at his expense with quips of his own.

The Soviet leader, as usual, also used the meal as an opportunity to push agenda items not yet addressed at the day's plenary session. He spoke repeatedly of the need to carve off a portion of Germany and give it to Poland, extending the latter's frontiers westward to the Oder River. He also renewed his arguments that the French empire be dismantled and France treated, essentially, as a conquered Axis nation rather than a liberated Allied one.

The most infamous moment of the dinner arrived when Stalin finally found a joke capable of getting under Churchill's skin. The Soviet leader said that the entire German military machine depended on around 50,000 officers, and that shooting these men – or perhaps 100,000 – out of hand would end German militarism. Given that the Soviets had done much the same with the cold-blooded slaughter of 22,000 Polish officers at the Katyn Massacre in 1940, this jest represented something Stalin might actually have ordered without a qualm. Whether he intended to sound out the reaction of the Western Allies to such a plan under cover of a joke, or simply wanted to annoy Churchill, cannot be determined, but Churchill responded that he could never countenance the barbarity of mass executions of men who only sought to fight for the sake of their country.

Nevertheless, Stalin did not stop his needling, as Churchill recounted: "Stalin however, perhaps only in mischief, pursued the subject. 'Fifty thousand,' he   said, 'must be shot.' I was deeply angered. 'I would rather,' I said, 'be taken out into the garden here and now and be shot myself than sully my own and my country's honour by such infamy.'" (Churchill, 2002, 454).

Roosevelt tried to defuse the situation by rendering it absurd, suggesting, tongue in cheek, that the Allies could shoot 49,000 Germans as a compromise figure. Sir Anthony Eden tried to calm Churchill also. However, at that moment, Roosevelt's newly arrived son, Elliot, showing a young man's inexperience, rose and stated with apparent seriousness that he supported Stalin's plan wholeheartedly. At this, Churchill strode out of the dining room, going to stand by himself in a darkened room adjacent to it. Overcome by rage and disgust at the idea and Elliot's apparently sincere endorsement of the proposal, the prime minister could endure no more for the moment. However, as he later described, "I had not been there a minute before hands were clapped upon my shoulders from behind, and there was Stalin, with Molotov at his side, both grinning broadly, and eagerly declaring that they were only playing, and that nothing of a serious character had entered their heads." (Churchill, 2002, 455).

Churchill suspected, probably accurately, that Stalin actually used the joke to "sound the waters" for Allied acceptance of mass executions of Germans. Nevertheless, the Soviet generalissimo ceased harassing Churchill, instead directing all his charm towards the prime minister. The Englishman permitted the Russians to calm him and returned to share the rest of the meal in a pleasantly festive atmosphere.

Churchill and Stalin

Chapter 6: November 30

Negotiations on the third day of the Eureka Summit, Churchill's 69th birthday, took a complex turn. The military committee meeting occurred earlier than decided the day before, at 9:30 AM rather than 10:30 AM, to give time to produce results Roosevelt could present to Stalin.

At noon, Roosevelt met with Reza Shah Pahlavi, the Shah-an-Shah of Iran. A pair of simultaneous tripartite lunches occurred at 1:30 PM – one involving Roosevelt, Churchill, and Stalin, and the other, held completely separately by prior agreement, bringing together the three nation's foreign ministers, Hopkins, Eden, and Molotov. Finally, the third plenary meeting occurred at 4 PM, followed by dinner at the British legation – and Winston Churchill's birthday party.

The Shah and Churchill

Once again, Sir Alan Brooke launched the military committee's meeting. This time, however, only Anglo-American military personnel attended. Voroshilov did not appear at this conference. Leahy, Brooke, Marshall, and Cunningham discussed the latest date that the critical 68 LSTs (Landing Ship Tanks) could remain for Italian operations. Considering that the ships would need repairs and refitting, the four men decided that the LSTs would leave the Mediterranean for England no later than February 1st.

Leahy pointed out that most of the arguments with the Soviets centered around the British refusal to agree to a firm May 1944 date for the D-Day landings. The night before, Harry Hopkins went to the British legation at Roosevelt's order, urging the prime minister to simply accept the May date with a "good grace." Apparently, these words took effect, for Brooke and Cunningham agreed to a three-point statement:

a. That we should continue to advance in Italy to the Pisa–Rimini line. [...] **b.** That an operation shall be mounted against the South of France on as big a scale as landing craft permit. For planning purposes D–day to be the same as Overlord D–day. [...] **c.** To recommend to the President and Prime Minister respectively that we should inform Marshal Stalin that we will launch Overlord during May." (Franklin, 1961, 959).

Reza Shah Pahlavi appeared at noon, accompanied by Minister of the Imperial Court Hussein

Ala, along with the Iranian Minister of Foreign Affairs and Prime Minister. No detailed record of the meeting survives, though Roosevelt apparently offered guarantees of postwar Iranian independence and economic aid.

The Shah

The Big Three met for lunch at 1:30 PM, the first tripartite meeting before a plenary session to occur at the summit. Roosevelt opened the session with the three-point agreement worked out earlier by the British and American military men. This pleased Stalin immensely, who now had a document clearly stating that Overlord would occur in May 1944 and that the Mediterranean operations would not delay it. Knowing it represented an important point to the Soviet strongman, FDR also promised that he would appoint a supreme commander for Operation Overlord immediately after he and Churchill returned to Cairo for the second part of their conference. This, too, worked out to Stalin's great satisfaction.

The three powerful leaders also briefly discussed Russia's access to warm water ports. Churchill promised to pressure Turkey to grant Russia free use of the Dardanelles, and, though not warm-water, Roosevelt noted that he wanted to make the Baltic freely accessible to all the major nations, the Soviet Union included. The atmosphere finally achieved a good deal of cordiality, with the main issue apparently settled.

At the "foreign ministers' lunch" attended by Eden, Molotov, Hopkins, and their interpreters, Molotov marveled over the fact that France could escape punishment for its collaboration with the Germans, echoing the theme raised repeatedly by Stalin. In response, Harry Hopkins pointed out Belgium and Holland also offered little resistance to the Germans, but that they, like France, had no capacity for effective resistance. Molotov expounded on Stalin's thesis that France willingly joined and helped the Axis, but then diverted the conversation to Stalin's idea of "strong points," suggesting one at Bizerte and another at Dakar. Eden suggested one in Belgium. These strong points would include military units and airbases from the nearest of the "Four Policemen," with those in the Atlantic area falling to the British and Americans to man and maintain.

The ministers turned next to the issue of Turkey, which Molotov found unsatisfactory, expecting the Turkish leader would refuse to join the war. Finally, the three men discussed sending aid to Tito in Yugoslavia, by which time the third plenary session approached rapidly, so Eden, Molotov, and Hopkins ended their meal.

Following the arguments of the first two plenary sessions, the third appeared nearly as an anticlimax. Roosevelt immediately repeated the three-point military statement in order to enter it in the official minutes and to inform the men not present at either the military conference or the Big Three's lunch of the situation. Roosevelt emphasized that Overlord would occur in May, with a strong simultaneous attack in southern France to support it, in accordance with the strategies discussed earlier.

A brief discussion followed in which Roosevelt hinted that George C. Marshall would likely command Operation Overlord as Supreme Allied commander. None of those present appeared to consider that anyone else might be chosen for the role, given Marshall's experience, military skill, and complete freedom from political entanglements.

The English prime minister now suggested that the Allies postpone further military discussion until he and Roosevelt recommenced their conference at Cairo following the Tehran summit. The leaders concurred with this position, deciding to issue a communique to the world indicating they had reached military decisions of the highest importance. Churchill observed that in preparing the communique, "the note to be sounded was brevity, mystery, and a foretaste of impending doom for Germany." (Churchill, 2002, 466).

The communique read in part: "The common understanding which we have here reached guarantees that victory will be ours. […] No power on earth can prevent our destroying the German armies by land, their U-boats by sea, and their war plants from the air. Our attack will be relentless and increasing. […] We came here with hope and determination. We leave here, friends in fact, in spirit and in purpose." (Franklin, 1961, 1,069).

With this matter concluded, the day's session ended with an agreement to discuss political matters on the morrow. Until then, these had taken an unexpected back seat to the details of Operation Overlord and the Mediterranean argument.

The British legation hosted the dinner that night, particularly appropriately since Churchill celebrated his 69th birthday that day. However, before Stalin arrived, NKVD agents and soldiers swarmed into the legation, searching it from roof to basement for assassins, bombs, and other threats. Only once they completed the search did Stalin himself put in an appearance. 50 heavily armed NKVD troops stationed themselves at the doors and windows, accompanied by a contingent of American military police. Stalin arrived with an additional armed bodyguard.

All of the Big Three proved to be in excellent spirits, relaxed and outgoing after their successful resolution of the Overlord wrangle. Roosevelt gave Churchill a magnificent antique Persian vase his men had acquired in the city as a birthday gift, and it remained one of the prime minister's prize possessions for the rest of his life.

Charles Bohlen later painted a vivid impression of the proceedings: "The table was set with British elegance. The crystal and silver sparkled in the candlelight. The amount of vodka and other alcohol consumed was large, although the three principals drank relatively little. Even in such a warm environment, Stalin could not resist a jab at Churchill." (Bohlen, 1973, 149).

Other attendees gave Churchill gifts. A cake with 69 candles had been provided. The guests dined on cheese soufflé, boiled salmon trout, turkey, and soup, while quaffing fine wines (or, in the case of Stalin, vodka, consumed neat). The Soviet dictator initially seemed daunted by the elaborate place setting and asked the translator Arthur Birse for help in choosing which utensils to use. However, he soon relaxed and started to enjoy the feast.

Churchill, despite Stalin's occasional attempts at a "putdown," entered fully into the birthday spirit and even went so far as to dance. Mike Reilly, the Secret Service chief, made a pertinent observation on the third night's dinner, describing it as "a party which the prime minister stole by dancing a gay and abandoned hornpipe. I think in the course of this story I have made it quite clear that, if the P. M. danced on his sixty-ninth birthday, it was because he felt like dancing, not because alcohol was asserting any undue influence. They just don't make that much alcohol." (Reilly, 1947,181).

Sir Alan Brooke, angered by Stalin's opening snub at Churchill and living up to his reputation as an excitable Irishman, waited for some time to allow his temper to cool. Then he turned and spoke to Stalin directly, with Birse interpreting. Brooke remarked first that he might have formed an incorrectly negative opinion of the Soviets due to their alliance with Hitler's Nazi Germany early in the war. He stated that this probably represented no more than a piece of misdirection – a

"Soviet cover plan." Stalin, interested despite himself, replied cautiously that might have been the case.

Brooke developed his theme further. He spoke of how the Soviets used dummy aircraft and tanks to deceive the Germans about the location of a coming offensive. He then deftly turned the comparisons to his advantage, indicating that Stalin deceived himself about the true British intentions when it came to Overlord: "Well, Marshal, you have been misled by dummy tanks and dummy aeroplanes, and you have failed to observe those feelings of true friendship which I have for the Red Army, nor have you seen the feelings of genuine comradeship which I bear towards all its members." (Churchill, 2002, 470).

The Soviet dictator received this unusual toast in silence, with his dark brown eyes unreadable in an expressionless face. However, shortly afterward, he turned to Churchill and said he liked Brooke, admiring him as a man who "rang true" and stating that he wished to talk with the British officer.

Even though the Big Three had scarcely touched on the political matters confronting them due to the long impasse over Operation Overlord, a sense that important business had been concluded and the Tehran Conference represented a success pervaded the gathering. The guests at Churchill's birthday party also clearly seemed to recognize the summit approached its end. Roosevelt concluded the evening with a short, inspiring speech, which stated in part, "There has been discussion here tonight of our varying colors of political complexion. I like to think of this in terms of the rainbow. [...] we have proved here at Teheran that the varying ideals of our nations can come together in a harmonious whole [...] So as we leave this historic gathering, we can see in the sky, for the first time, that traditional symbol of hope, the rainbow." (Franklin, 1961, 987).

A picture of the Big Three during the birthday party

After this, the dinner party dispersed. Stalin left in his armored limousine with his cordon of guards, and Roosevelt returned to his own quarters at the Soviet legation. Only a single day now remained for the Tehran conference.

Chapter 7: The End of the Summit

The last day of the summit focused on political issues, including Poland, Finland, and the fate of Germany after the war. The Big Three met for a lunch in Roosevelt's quarters along with their foreign ministers (Eden, Hopkins, Molotov) and effectively started the day's negotiations there.

The first order of business at lunch consisted of drafting a telegram for dispatch to the Turkish president. This telegram asked him to meet Churchill and Roosevelt in Cairo following their return there, so that the Allies could attempt to bring Turkey into the war. Sir Anthony Eden opined that the best they might hope from the Turks consisted of the use of Anatolian airbases, and Churchill pledged to provide fighters and bombers for the project if the talks succeeded.

After Stalin agreed to send a representative to Cairo, Roosevelt broached the fact that he wanted Finland, then fighting against the USSR on the German side, to escape most consequences, continuing as a free, independent nation with little or no punishment. Stalin objected at first, saying the Finns could make reparations in kind for 6-8 years. However, Churchill backed up Roosevelt, and the Soviet leader said it would be a shame to deprive so courageous a people of their freedom, perhaps thinking that it would present no easy task against the tough, determined Finns, either.

Between lunch and the plenary session, Roosevelt managed to pull Stalin aside with only the translators Bohlen and Pavlov present. The president, to Bohlen's immense dismay, told Stalin that with another election coming up, he planned to run for a fourth term, and due to the presence of millions of Polish voters in the United States, he did not wish to speak about Poland at this time, lest he commit to some unpopular stance. Stalin accepted this windfall stoically, and the president and Soviet generalissimo joined the British prime minister around the green baize table for the final day of negotiations.

Roosevelt later recorded a bizarre incident in his own writings about an action he took at the very start of the final plenary session. According to his narrative, he deliberately mocked and humiliated Churchill in order to toady Stalin into becoming his friend and treat him as a "man and equal." "I began to tease Churchill about his Britishness, about John Bull, about his cigars, about his habits. It began to register with Stalin. Winston got red and scowled, and the more he did so, the more Stalin smiled. Finally Stalin broke out into a deep hearty guffaw, and for the first time in three days I saw light. I kept it up until Stalin was laughing with me, and it was then I called him 'Uncle Joe.'" (Perkins, 1946, 82-83).

Whether Roosevelt actually carried out the sophomoric mortification of his strongest ally in order to 'break the ice' with a hostile and contemptuous tyrant remains unknown. No other witness of the conference records this incident, either because it happened only in Roosevelt's imagination or due to embarrassment over FDR's behavior.

Stalin raised the first question on the day's agenda – the disposal of Italy's shipping now that the Italians had surrendered to the Allies. Both Roosevelt and Churchill readily agreed that the Soviet Union should have the use of the Italian vessels until the end of the war, after which they could be divided among the Allied powers. Churchill agreed to send the ships to the Black Sea if the Turks entered the war, allowing free passage of the Dardanelles, and otherwise to Russia's northern ports.

The next item up for discussion consisted of the fate of Poland. Roosevelt, true to his word, refrained from participating in this debate, playing the role of passive observer. Charles Bohlen seethed quietly in his seat at the president's side while this went on. Churchill and Stalin held a long discussion, during which Stalin stated that he wanted Russia's border to move west to the Curzon Line and to compensate Poland with a slice of eastern Germany. Initially, the two men tried to work out the details on a tiny map ripped out of a copy of the *Times* of London. However, Bohlen offered them an atlas in the possession of the Americans, and Stalin drew his proposed border changes using his habitually carried red pencil.

The question of Finland followed. Both Roosevelt and Churchill wanted Finland spared serious consequences as long as it broke with Germany and expelled any Germans on its territory, while Stalin held out for indemnities. Churchill responded that large indemnities did not work, that the Allies had larger matters to handle than shaking down the Finns, and that if he had been born a Soviet commissar, he would urge Stalin the same way – a notion which perhaps prompted a sardonic inward smile from the Soviet dictator.

The final item on the agenda consisted of Roosevelt's proposal to split Germany into five separate nations. Stalin tentatively supported the idea, while Churchill pointed out the weaknesses in the scheme.

The negotiations then wound down. Few issues found definite settlement, leading to another, even more confusing conference at Yalta in early 1945.

Stalin came away with the impression that Roosevelt supported his reconfiguration of Poland, when in fact the president merely intended to be evasive for electioneering purposes. The Western Allies had, however, secured some postwar protection for Finland, which fought alongside Germany out of well-founded fear of Soviet imperialism rather than dedication to Hitler's cause.

The participants left scant record of the tripartite dinner following. The American president meant to leave the following morning, since a major cold front forecast to arrive on December 3rd might otherwise render his departure difficult. At the dinner, the Big Three signed two documents. One, the "Declaration of the Three Powers on Iran," bombastically saluted Iran's sovereignty and the Allies' intention to give the country aid postwar, but it failed to provide a single concrete detail.

The other, the Military Agreement, included five points:

1. The Allies would aid Tito's Yugoslavian partisans.

2. The Allies would attempt to bring Turkey into the war.

3. The Soviet Union would declare war on Bulgaria if Turkey entered the war.

4. Operation Overlord would occur in May 1944 along with a secondary invasion in southern France. The Soviets pledged to begin a simultaneous offensive to prevent Hitler from shifting the full weight of his divisions westward.

5. The military staffs of the three Allies would keep in touch to coordinate from that point on, and attempt to work out a deception plan to cover Overlord.

With these matters settled, Roosevelt took his leave of the other two statesmen on the evening of December 1st. The American president traveled by car, escorted by Jeeps, to the US Army-held Camp Amirabad. There, the delegation's expectation of a restful time swiftly shattered as a heart attack nearly killed Roosevelt's friend General Edwin "Pa" Watson. Though Watson survived (to later die of a stroke while returning from the Yalta conference in early 1945), the Americans spent what Mike Reilly called a "rough night."

Watson (right) helping Roosevelt stand

The following day, the Big Three flew out of Tehran, Churchill and Roosevelt to Cairo and Stalin to Baku and his waiting armored train. While waiting in a Jeep on the runway, Admiral Leahy turned to Harry Hopkins and, referring to the Russians, said with a bitter smile, "Well, Harry, all I can say is, nice friends we have now." (Bohlen, 1973, 152). Roosevelt, however, exhibited a cheerful, optimistic mood, and even Churchill seemed pleased that a sort of military agreement had been hammered out and that it addressed his current fixation, that of bringing Turkey into the war.

Roosevelt and Churchill would return to Cairo to continue their conference in more detail and to meet with the president of Turkey, but for now, while the Tehran conference sowed the seeds for future disagreements about Polish borders, the fate of Germany, and other matters, it did make several important changes in the course of the war. Eureka cemented the Western Allied intention to launch Operation Dragoon, the invasion of southern France, in conjunction with D-

Day, a decision hastening the collapse of German resistance there. It enabled the Finns to avoid destruction by the Soviets, and FDR chose Dwight D. Eisenhower in place of the expected George C. Marshall to head the Overlord invasion, within a few days, just as Stalin asked. Lastly, it prompted Roosevelt to believe he had made a friend of Josef Stalin – a factor leading to unforeseen and major consequences for postwar Europe and the world.

The Yalta Conference

Chapter 1: The Strategic Situation

The situation in Europe during the latter days of World War II developed in a complex, non-linear fashion that determined the mirroring complexities – and general futility – of the Yalta Conference. On the Eastern Front, the Soviets, saved earlier in the war at the eleventh hour by massive Lend-Lease aid and Japan's decision to attack the Americans and British rather than open a second front in the USSR, now held a dominant position in much of Eastern Europe. Soviet forces, which had aided Hitler in dismembering democratic Poland a few years earlier, now held all of Polish territory, in addition to much of Eastern Europe north of the Balkans. Their acts of brutal repression, murder, terror, and forced deportation in Poland already made the Western Allies understandably suspicious of Soviet intentions. However, furious German resistance slowed the final drive into Germany proper.

In the West, American strategic decisions trumped British planning. Though certainty remains impossible, this likely prevented a total Soviet conquest of Germany and possibly France. The British aimed at a peripheral strategy, focusing on the Mediterranean and the Balkans, but the Americans, however, insisted on landings in Western Europe for the express purpose of not only crushing the Germans faster but of keeping the Soviets from establishing a more powerful Central European foothold. Given Stalin's intention of arranging a 10-year "breather" before launching further attacks on the hated capitalist world, and the contemptuous hostility his right-hand minion Vyacheslav Molotov expressed during a later assessment of Roosevelt's aims, expecting the worst from the violent military dictatorship of Soviet Russia appears to have been a sensible perspective among those American leaders who held it.

Гребованне Председателя Совнаркома СССР и Народного Комиссара Иностранных Дел тов. В. М. Молотова в Берлине. На снимке — т. В. М. Молотов и г. А. Гитлер в новой имперской канцелярии. Фото М. Калашникова.

Molotov and Hitler before the war

The Soviet Union, in fact, remained a nakedly imperialistic power every bit as brutal and aggressive as the Third Reich. In 1920, the Soviets attempted to overrun Poland in order to invade Germany, weakened by the First World War, and make it the centerpiece of an all-conquering "Red" empire. Only a stunning defeat by the Poles under the skilled leadership of Marshal Poniatowksi, and the simultaneous defeat of communist uprisings in Germany by vicious but effective right-wing paramilitaries, baffled this first attempt.

During the intervening years, the Soviet Union carried out various unabashed attacks against neighboring countries. The conquered Ukraine suffered through brutal purges and a genocidal, deliberately engineered famine which likely killed at least 3 million people, as the Soviets sought to break the independent spirit of the stubborn, combative Ukrainians.

The USSR also joined readily with Nazi Germany in order to seize the coveted Baltic states and part of Poland. During this period, the Gestapo and NKVD even held several meetings to coordinate political repression and murder in their respective Polish satrapies.

Following World War II, the continuing aggression of the Soviets would emerge in numerous incidents. The siege of Berlin, thwarted by the Berlin Airlift, showed Russian willingness to violate treaty terms in the interest of further aggrandizing their territory. And though they were cautious about triggering a direct confrontation with the powerful United States, particularly after Harold S. Truman's nuclear "warning shots" at Hiroshima and Nagasaki, the Soviets nevertheless launched a "fifth column" assault westward in the postwar years by fomenting communist revolutions in Greece and, abortively, in Italy and Austria. The Soviet Union also used proxies such as North Korea and North Vietnam to test American resolve or demonstrate American "weakness" in an effort to detach allies from the Western camp.

In light of this dedicated hostility, betraying a strongly predatory motive on the USSR's part over the course of decades, America's decision to advance quickly into Germany after the Battle of the Bulge appears to have been a prudent step for preserving the Free World – and far less costly than a separate war to oust triumphant Soviets from Western Europe. In tandem with that, once they were partly independent of Hitler's increasingly crazed commands, German commanders assessed the situation and formed a rough but workable strategy; correctly deeming defeat by the Western Allies the lesser of two evils compared to Soviet conquest, the Germans fought desperately to delay the Soviets as much as possible in the East, not hoping to win but to slow Stalin's armies sufficiently to keep them off most of German soil.

Of course, the Wehrmacht did not abandon its struggle against the Anglo-American forces, either. With the paradoxical behavior often seen in humans, the Germans also fought with the fury of a cornered beast against the Western Allies, slowing the advance of the very people they hoped might preserve part of Germany from Russian seizure. In this, the threat of the Morgenthau Plan (which proposed the complete demolition of Germany's economy) and President Roosevelt's possibly ill-advised insistence on unconditional surrender (mostly designed for the probably redundant purpose of preventing a late-war peace or alliance between the USSR and the Third Reich) likely played a role in the German army's somewhat schizophrenic response to impending defeat – along with military pride, patriotism, and simple defiance.

This, then, represented the strategic situation when the leaders known as the Big Three gathered for the Yalta Conference. The Soviet Union already held most of the territory it had no intention of relinquishing for the next 45 years, the British remained obsessed with the Balkans, and the Americans wavered between Roosevelt's astonishing faith in Stalin's benevolent intentions and a hard-headed, pragmatic understanding of the need to keep Germany intact and as free as possible of communist dominance. As a final ingredient in the negotiations, the Germans – naturally with no representative present, but the main subject on the agenda nevertheless – maintained a despairing but lethal rearguard action that also influenced the three leaders' decisions.

The personal character, strengths, and weaknesses of the three men gathering to make a pretense at deciding Europe's future – a future already much determined by the juggernaut of circumstance – gave the Yalta Conference some of its unique color and interest. Each represented one of the foremost statesmen of his nation's history, a truly remarkable individual who left his stamp on events despite the Conference's overall futility.

The most transparent of the three chief participants, Winston Churchill, left the clearest impressions of his thought processes to history. His speeches, numerous letters, and voluminous memoirs, taken with British government communications, create a fairly complete picture of his shifting perceptions and purposes. At the time of Yalta, Churchill wanted to preserve Britain not only as an independent nation, but as a first-rate world power. He dreaded being reduced to a minor player caught between the Soviet Union and the United States, though he greatly preferred the USA to the USSR. To this end, he wanted to preserve the British Empire, ensuring Britain a reasonable degree of clout in the postwar world. How to do so ultimately eluded even his formidable if eccentric intellect.

Up to Yalta, Churchill and the British government carried out bilateral negotiations with the USSR, leaving the Americans out totally. While Churchill relied profoundly on his New World allies for military success, he preferred to settle the disposition of Europe with other Europeans. Swallowing his bitter hatred of communism and deep, well-merited suspicions of Stalin's motives, he and other British statesmen sought to hammer out an Anglo-Soviet accord.

At the heart of Churchill's thinking lay the division of Europe into British and Soviet spheres of influence. He conceived of these spheres as areas of diplomatic and commercial involvement, not direct imperial command. Like the rest of the British, he obsessed over retaining influence in the Balkans, lying as they did on the doorstep of British Empire possessions in the Levant and the strategically crucial Eastern Mediterranean.

During these dealings, Churchill showed an alarming readiness to sacrifice the Poles as the price for gaining a peace favorable to the British Empire's survival. He even expressed annoyance tat protests by the Polish government in exile at the handing-off of their unfortunate nation from one totalitarian conqueror to another. While Roosevelt and later Truman were very concerned about the post-war Soviet Union, Russian undertakings at Yalta, particularly with respect to Poland, were accepted by Churchill at face value. During the subsequent parliamentary debate, comparisons were made with the debacle that transpired at Munich only six years earlier. Yet it would have been impossible for Churchill to publicly disown the deal: doing so would have snuffed out the possibility, however remote, that some kind of pluralism would be tolerated in Soviet-occupied Poland.

In Churchill's favor, however, weighed the fact that the Nazis and then the Soviets actually controlled Poland. In the Hobbesian universe of international warfare and politics, possession represented more than nine-tenths of the law. Stonily immune to appeals to conscience or fairness, the Soviets could only be dislodged from Poland by a military force Britain did not possess. Churchill, in effect, gave up what he had already lost in the hopes of gaining Stalin's cooperation.

As this predicament should make clear, Churchill occupied an unenviable position. The war had nearly finished England as a military power, and the American economic colossus threatened the older nation's commercial preeminence. In effect, the Prime Minister had almost nothing to offer, yet he remained obliged by patriotic considerations to try to carve out a place for England as a continuing global superpower with little more than his own charisma.

President Franklin Roosevelt represents either a more enigmatic figure, or one of almost shocking transparency. Feeble, emaciated, half-crippled, and slowly dying, Roosevelt radiated physical frailty and mental detachment. Outwardly, he continually professed a desire to make Stalin his "friend," and achieve an amicable understanding with the Soviets. He listened to some degree at least to the optimistic men in his administration who thought Russia would become a close trading partner with the United States.

On the other hand, Roosevelt often showed himself a realist despite his underlying ethical core, and he proved quite skilled at bluff or at concealing his actual purposes until the last minute. Roosevelt may have been a dying man desperate for a touch of human warmth in a cold world, his reason subordinated to an overwhelming desire for lasting peace that overcame any reservations about Stalin and the Soviets. Alternatively, he might have continued playing the game, feigning enthusiastic friendliness towards his ominous allies in order to allay their suspicions and win the Westerners more time to prepare against any postwar Soviet aggression.

One certainty at least emerges from Roosevelt's actions at the time of Yalta – his absolute determination to create the United Nations as a bulwark for future peace. President Woodrow Wilson attempted the same at the end of World War I, creating the League of Nations. However, the United States failed to join the organization and the League remained toothless and futile in the period between the two wars. Thus, Roosevelt wanted to create the United Nations as an improved version of the League, headed by the United States, the United Kingdom, the Soviet Union, and Chiang Kai-Shek's Nationalist China. Though many other countries would hold seats in the UN, Roosevelt envisioned these four as holding the senior position, making them able to pressure the other countries (and each other) into avoiding conflict-generating situations. The UN headquarters would be in the United States, increasing the organization's authority with the military and industrial power of America.

The final member of this weirdly assorted troika, Soviet Premier Josef Stalin, was and is the most opaque of the three men. A dangerous, highly ambitious dictator, Stalin systematically destroyed most records relating to his decisions and decision-making process, so that even the opening of the Soviet archives revealed little more about his purposes than might be observed from the outside. He also conducted a large part of his governing via telephone calls, rather than through letters, memorandums, or written orders. This quite deliberate policy left no fixed record of his intentions, enabling him to easily change or disavow his commands and remain an ever-present, powerful, yet ghostly and elusive presence in Soviet politics.

Such indications of Stalin's purposes that remain reveal that he knew he was holding most of the trump cards at the end of the war. He already held a large slice of Europe, an area where he had no intention of permitting self-determination, and the former Nazi colonies would now become Soviet colonies, the spoils of war. Stalin's few surviving declarations on the topic indicate that he viewed the Eastern European acquisitions as a "buffer zone." However, this would only continue for the next decade or so, after which the Soviet Union would be sufficiently rebuilt to renew the struggle against capitalism. While not explicitly including an invasion plan, these words seem to indicate long-term hostile intent towards Western Europe and the United States. As a result, most of Stalin's participation in the Yalta Conference consisted of him reaffirming the existing position of the USSR as the de facto owner of Eastern Europe.

Chapter 2: Arranging the Yalta Conference

Stalin, ever paranoid and possibly fearing a coup if he left the Soviet Union for too long, refused to leave his own territory for this second conference between the three chief Allied leaders. Unwilling to travel as far as Casablanca in North Africa, the Soviet strongman left the negotiations there to Churchill and Roosevelt. The next summit, at Tehran in 1943, occurred at a venue Stalin proved willing to visit. At that meeting, the Big Three heads of state laid rather vague plans for dividing Germany into multiple small states, its condition prior to Chancellor Otto von Bismarck's founding of the German Empire in 1871. However, the overall effect of this summit left Germany's fate undecided, with further complications added as Churchill and Free French leader Charles de Gaulle visited Moscow in 1944 to negotiate directly with Stalin.

De Gaulle

Churchill initiated the Yalta Conference in response to the uncertain future of Germany and his deep concerns about Soviet imperial ambitions in Poland and other Eastern European countries. He also suggested the codename Operation Argonaut to conceal the plan from potential assassins, while perhaps invoking a quest in search of the "Golden Fleece" of a peaceful settlement of the increasingly tense Allied situation.

Initially, the British Prime Minister suggested a meeting in September 1944 in northern Scotland, but Stalin, wanting to postpone the meeting until he had seized most of the territory he wanted, turned this idea down flat. Undeterred, Roosevelt proposed an Alaskan meeting, but Stalin again refused, offering to send Vyacheslav Molotov in his place.

When the two other Allied leaders continued to press him, the Soviet dictator eventually agreed to meet, offering the Black Sea ports as the venue. American officials studied the matter and finally picked Yalta, mostly due to their belief that it remained undamaged by the war and their assessment of a pleasant winter climate unlikely to overstress the system of their sickly president. Roosevelt took their recommendation and wrote a letter to Churchill in December 1944: "If Stalin cannot manage to meet us in the Mediterranean I am prepared to come to the Crimea and have the meeting at Yalta, which appears to be the best place   available in the Black Sea, having the best accommodations ashore and the most   promising flying conditions." (Churchill, 1953, 401).

With no intercontinental aircraft available at the time (the first designs languished on Third Reich drafting tables for want of resources), Roosevelt would travel by sea to reach the rendezvous. Stopping at Malta, he would fly from there to Yalta, though his failing heart meant the aircraft would need to remain dangerously low to avoid overstressing his system and killing him outright.

For his part, Churchill suggested sending a few destroyers on to Malta to serve as floating housing if the Soviets failed to provide acceptable quarters. He also proposed meeting Roosevelt in Malta before going on to the site of Operation Argonaut. A literate man with a flair for words and a quirky sense of humor, the British Prime Minister could not resist a pun in the addendum to the message he sent on New Year's Day 1945: "We shall be delighted if you will come to Malta. I shall be waiting on the quay. You will also see the inscription of your noble message to Malta of a year ago.   Everything can be arranged to your convenience. No more let us falter! From Malta to Yalta! Let nobody alter!" (Churchill, 1953, 402)

Stalin naturally agreed to the meeting on his turf, particularly since he could travel by train from Moscow directly to the location using the personal luxury railcar of the late Czar Nicolas II. At that time, the dictator seemed quite averse to flying, though whether due to fear of crashing, German interception, assassination by sabotage, or a mix of these concerns, remains unknown.

Churchill wanted to carry out a separate bilateral summit (far more informally, but perhaps just as crucially) on Malta before flying on to the Crimea. Though he urged this with great persistence, Roosevelt turned him down every time, citing the extremely tight timetable. The American president also refused to send his Secretary of State, the Connecticut-born Edward Stettinius, Jr. He did, however, dispatch his most trusted adviser, Harry Hopkins, then gradually dying of stomach cancer, to consult with the English statesman.

Stettinius

Hopkins

Stalin traveled to the Crimea by train, enjoying the easiest journey of the three despite the condition of the Soviet Union following German devastation. Churchill flew from Northolt to Malta on January 29th, 1945, with his close advisers and staff aboard a trio of aircraft. His daughter Sarah also accompanied him, in a curious echo of Roosevelt's official Argonaut party. While Churchill's aircraft arrived safely, one of the three planes crashed into the sea, killing all but five of the people on board. The sudden death of secretaries and advisers known to Churchill and his party for years chilled the British with awareness of the dangers besetting their trip, not merely from hostile action but also random accidents.

Roosevelt's journey proved the most difficult for several reasons. His trip to Yalta represented the longest by far, and his alarmingly fragile condition made the plain process of traveling internationally potentially fatal even without other hazards. Overwhelming Allied air dominance made attacks on Churchill's aircraft or Stalin's train unlikely, but vengeful U-boats still lurked in the Atlantic and Mediterranean, and, in a surface ship, Roosevelt would be in easy reach of their torpedoes.

The Americans made elaborate efforts to conceal Roosevelt's departure from the United States, partly baffled by the inquisitiveness of a free press only patchily reined in by wartime censorship. Roosevelt appeared at his inauguration to announce the start of his unprecedented fourth term as president, making a very short fourth inaugural address to conceal his almost total physical collapse. However, he did include a reference to the upcoming negotiations and the methods he intended to apply during them: "We have learned that we must live as men, not as ostriches, [...] We have learned the simple truth, as Emerson said, that 'The only way to have a friend is to be one.' We can gain no lasting peace if we approach it with suspicion and mistrust or with fear. We can gain it only if we proceed with the understanding, the confidence, and the courage which flow from conviction." (Manis, 1998, 294).

An upcoming conference between Roosevelt, Stalin, and Churchill constituted common knowledge in January 1945. However, the Allies successfully concealed both the summit's time and location, even as incautious American naval crews and the ever-inquisitive press nearly managed to reveal the details immediately before Roosevelt's voyage. The Baltimore-class heavy cruiser USS *Quincy* served as Roosevelt's transport. Seven destroyers and nine cruisers formed the *Quincy*'s formidable escort when it left Newport News, Virginia, while several other vessels joined the presidential convoy en route. Roosevelt's wife Eleanor began filling in for her husband at official receptions several weeks before the January 23rd launch of the convoy, helping to further obscure the precise date when the president left the safety of American shores.

The USS *Quincy*

Eleanor

The party included several key advisers and other personnel, including Alger Hiss. The infamous Hiss already worked for the Soviets as a spy, according to the records declassified with the fall of the Soviet Union. However, his military handlers gave him no specific instructions regarding the Yalta Conference, and all evidence suggests that Hiss maintained his cover by discharging his duties with apparent faithfulness, making no attempt to alter the course of the negotiations.

Just as Churchill brought his daughter to the summit, so Roosevelt brought his own daughter, Anna Roosevelt Boettiger, as a confidante, adviser, and helper. Boettiger, a strong personality in her own right, possessed considerable unofficial influence over the president and also left a valuable account of the Yalta meeting. The March 5th, 1945 issue of *Time* magazine ran an extensive, laudatory feature on her and her role at Yalta: "Actually Franklin Roosevelt couldn't have asked for a better companion. Anna is happy-natured and golden-haired, and her tall, bony figure is good to look upon. Her energy is so prodigious that she can plan a [...] movie party [...] at the White House with a full day's work handling her father's affairs. More dependable than her brothers, she once evoked the remark from Jim Farley that 'Anna has the most political savvy of all the Roosevelt children.' [...] Free-speaking and free-cussing, she holds her opinions lightly and expects others to do the same." (Chamberlain, 1945, 100-102).

Eleanor and Anna

Another key individual, Admiral William D. Leahy, an Iowa-born naval man who spent his childhood in the small Wisconsin port city of Ashland on Lake Superior, furnished advice to Roosevelt on military matters, officially bearing the title Chief of Staff to the Commander in Chief. A long-faced man with something of the look of a stereotypical Irish policeman from a 1940s crime drama, the canny, experienced Leahy advised both Roosevelt and his successor Harry S. Truman.

Leahy

Roosevelt's notion of bringing 35 people to the summit represented a gross underestimate. Together, the Anglo-American delegation numbered over 700, and included a roll call of famous names from the World War II era, called together to confer on the future of Europe and the world.

Roosevelt's voyage took 11 days, during which time the frail President fell ill with a cold. Churchill, meanwhile, also found himself stricken down by illness – a stark reminder that just a few generations ago, even the most powerful had no access to the medical treatments common in the 21st century. Both had to spend considerable "downtime" due to ailments later doctors could suppress, medicate, or cure.

On February 2nd, 1945, the USS *Quincy* entered Valetta Harbor. The Maltese citizenry turned out in great numbers to cheer as the ship glided over the dark blue water. Roosevelt managed to come up on deck and prop himself in a chair to enjoy the warmth and brilliant sunlight of the morning, as well as the pleasant island views. Churchill, almost incapacitated by a high fever, waited on the HMS *Orion* rather than on the quay as originally planned. The British played the Star-Spangled Banner to greet their New World allies, and the Americans responded with God Save the Queen, moving both Churchill and Anthony Eden deeply despite their uncertainty about American attitudes.

Eden

By lunchtime, Churchill rallied enough to join Roosevelt for a meal on board the *Quincy*. The two statesmen's daughters, Sarah Oliver and Anna Roosevelt Boettiger, lunched with their two aging, ailing fathers, meeting for the first time and making a favorable impression upon one another. British official Anthony Eden, U.S. Admiral Leahy, and other prominent men also attended. The Americans went to great lengths to make Churchill feel welcome, including supplying him with cigars and a candle to light them with, his favorite method as opposed to a lighter.

After the lunch, the British government officials proved eager to discuss the upcoming meeting and plan a joint strategy. However, Roosevelt refused point blank to cooperate. To the alarm and distress of Churchill, Eden, and other senior English leaders, the American president left the *Quincy* after a pleasant, joke-filled chat and spent the rest of the day as a tourist, ambling about and viewing both the magnificent vistas and the horrendous damage left by earlier German bombing.

This action provides a likely insight into Roosevelt's thoughts, indicating his belief he could make a friend out of the lethal, sphinx-like Stalin was probably genuine, and not a mere pose. Roosevelt wanted to avoid conferring with Churchill before the summit so that Stalin would not think the two Western Allies colluded against him. This well-meaning but decidedly naïve approach backfired doubly: not only did Roosevelt squander the chance to talk with Churchill before the three-way meeting, but the Soviets also refused to believe the American's assurances that no such scheming had taken place, so Roosevelt's gesture won him no political capital whatsoever with the hard, paranoid men on Stalin's staff.

Churchill, Roosevelt, Eden, Stettinius, and other key members of both delegations gathered on the *Quincy* again in the evening for dinner. Finally, Churchill managed to turn the conversation briefly to political matters. Stettinius, an energetic, perspicacious individual, helped summarize the preliminary discussions he had conducted with the British. However, dinner proved too short for the detailed consultation Churchill wanted.

After eating, the concourse of 700 officials and staff boarded aircraft, where many of them – including Churchill and Roosevelt – lay down to sleep during the flight to Crimea's Saki Airfield. The airplanes took off at intervals of ten minutes, and the flight proved miserable for all involved due to the cold. Additionally, Roosevelt's aircraft flew very low to prevent altitude stress on the president, but this measure exposed it to brutal turbulence, meaning Roosevelt, Boettiger, and his close advisers barely slept.

The aircraft landed on Saki Airfield the next morning, finding it covered in deep snow, a chilly contrast to the pleasant Mediterranean warmth of Malta. The two leaders inspected a Soviet honor guard awaiting them, then boarded a fleet of waiting cars for an eight-hour drive to Yalta. Along the way, Vyacheslav Molotov, playing the role of master of ceremonies with expansive relish, arranged a series of splendidly catered gourmet meals for the visiting dignitaries. Somewhat more ominously, Churchill noted thousands of Soviet soldiers, both male and female, gathered at the roadside in silent battalions, watching the cavalcade as it drove past, likely serving both to mark the momentousness of the occasion and provide an enormous security cordon for Stalin himself.

Chapter 3: Yalta

Roosevelt and Churchill aboard a ship at Yalta

Yalta, though located in an ideal location for a seaside resort town, bore the wounds of German occupation and demolition when the Big Three appeared there in 1945. Most of the buildings had suffered damage or were entirely leveled, bomb craters pocked the ground, and the Germans and local looters stripped the larger buildings of every stick of furniture, fixture, and convenience.

Nevertheless, the Soviets pulled out all stops to prepare several buildings in suitable style for the visiting dignitaries and the conference. Two czarist era palaces in Yalta provided lodgings for the American and Soviet delegations respectively, while the British received a large manor house five miles away in Alupka. The Russians assigned the largest and best palace, the Livadia Palace, to Roosevelt and his staff; this locale also provided the venue for the meetings, in deference to the American president's frailty.

The Big Three at the Livadia Palace

Stalin and his aides and bodyguards occupied the slightly more modest Yusupov Palace, while Churchill and the British occupied the Vorontsov Palace. This mansion, built by the English architects Edward Blore and William Hunt in the first half of the 19th century for Prince Mikhail Semyonovich Vorontsov, features a startling mishmash of Gothic, Scottish, and Mogul architectural elements. Though slightly less magnificent than the Livadia and Yusupov Palaces, the location pleased Churchill greatly, as he recorded in his memoirs: "The setting of our abode was impressive. Behind the villa, half Gothic and half Moorish in style, rose the mountains, covered in snow [...] Before us lay the dark expanse of the Black Sea, severe, but still agreeable and warm even at this time of the year. Carved white lions guarded the entrance to the house, and beyond the courtyard lay a fine park with sub-tropical plants and cypresses." (Churchill, 1953, 412).

Derevyagin Igor's picture of the Vorontsov Palace

The liveable conditions, in fact, resulted from massive efforts on the Soviets' part. A thousand men had been deployed to repair and refit the Vorontsov palace alone, with larger numbers involved in the restoration of the other two palaces. Part of the process involved clearing the extensive minefields the Germans left behind. Churchill's party received warnings not to leave the Vorontsov's grounds due to adjacent uncleared minefields where a strolling band of British peers could easily have come to grief.

With the palaces emptied entirely, Stalin deputed Lavrentiy Beria to prepare them suitably for use. Beria, in turn, assigned the task to two men, the construction expert Leon Safrazyan and the NKVD general Sergei Kruglov. Kruglov's NKVD thugs brought a swarm of POWs, mostly Romanians, to work as slave labor, while Safrazyan mustered his Soviet work crews and the local people. A contingent of soldiers and NKVD men descended on the large Moscow hotels, stripping them of furniture, lighting, carpets, and even sinks, toilets, bathtubs, and plumbing. The men packed all of these items on railcars for dispatch to the Crimea. With a flood of construction supplies and plundered furnishings flooding into Yalta, and practically unlimited labor available, Kruglov and Safrazyan metamorphosed the three palaces in the span of just three weeks before the arrival of the Big Three.

Kathleen Harriman of the American delegation recalled that the NKVD's interior decorators still fussed over the details of décor after Roosevelt's arrival: "The rugs for the President's suite have been changed four times. Each time all the furniture had to be moved out — and it's big and heavy and Victorian. The Soviets just couldn't make up their minds which oriental colors looked best." (Plokhy, 2010, 65).

The Soviets provided their guests with every luxury that a totalitarian government could supply on short notice, which were considerable. Like Martin Bormann attending to Hitler's whims to the extent of planting shade trees overnight or eradicating farms to improve the Fuhrer's view, the Soviets spared no effort to lavish care on their guests: "On one occasion Portal had admired a large glass tank with plants growing in it, and remarked that it contained no fish. Two days later a consignment of goldfish arrived. Another time somebody said casually that there was no lemon peel in the cocktails. The next day a lemon tree loaded with fruit was growing in the hall. All must have come by air from far away." (Churchill, 1953, 413).

The luxury of the palaces contrasted starkly to the ruin surrounding them. The town of Yalta itself consisted of the roofless shells of houses. The husks of burned-out tanks and bombed trains dotted the landscape. A considerable portion of the damage occurred at Soviet hands, as the communists deported the independence-minded Crimean Tartars by the hundreds of thousands in 1944. The Soviets used so much secrecy and repression, however, that none of the Anglo-Americans knew this and thought the deserted towns they saw had been depopulated by the Germans.

Despite the almost fawning care given to the foreigners in their quarters, the visitors soon discovered a frightening hostility and paranoia lay beneath the smiling surface of waiters, servants, and English-speaking officers who catered to the guests' requirements. Hordes of Soviet guards filled the grounds and streets, preventing the delegations from straying beyond a few areas approved for walking. Moroever, suspicious, heavily armed soldiers demanded identity papers even from prominent individuals at frequent intervals. In particular, the Soviets did their best to prevent all contact between the Westerners and the local people. Those few locals permitted to interact with the Americans and British knew enough to keep their mouths shut beyond a few bland pleasantries.

A more sinister effort occurred at the same time, of which the Anglo-American delegation remained in complete ignorance. While Churchill admired his goldfish and Roosevelt enjoyed fresh caviar and champagne, NKVD agents scrutinized the local population (as secret documents declassified after the fall of the Soviet Union revealed) and arrested 835 people for "looking suspicious."

As the final piece of Soviet misdirection, Stalin and Molotov played a "good cop, bad cop" routine at Yalta. Molotov – actually Stalin's puppet – took the role of a hard-line, demanding negotiator. Stalin, meanwhile, played the part of a mild, liberal, avuncular figure, inclined to be accommodating but forced to take a harder line by Molotov's intransigence. The deception successfully hoodwinked both Churchill and Roosevelt.

Chapter 4: The Negotiations

Though Churchill naturally hoped to occupy an equal role in the Yalta Conference, the leading positions of the Soviets and Americans appeared from the beginning. In effect, this echoed the actual military roles of the three powers. The Soviets mustered the Allies' biggest land army, while the Americans deployed a smaller but still formidable land force and occupied the premier role in naval and air operations by war's end. Britain acted in a supplemental role to the United States, simply lacking the manpower or industrial muscle to retain full strategic parity.

American and Soviet negotiators, therefore, met late on February 3rd to set the agenda for the first talks on the following day. Molotov represented the Russians, while Averell Harriman and Charles Bohlen (Roosevelt's personal interpreter) spoke for the American side. The men came to a surprisingly easy agreement, setting the first three-way summit meeting for 5 PM. They chose Livadia Palace as the venue due to Roosevelt's illness, and the Soviets accepted Roosevelt's dinner invitation to Stalin after the meeting.

Harriman

The first night in Yalta proved a mix of unexpected luxury and occasionally startling moments of squalor: "The servants, the silver, the glassware, the vodka, the carpets and hangings, 'the gilt furniture,' as Churchill's physician Lord Moran put it, 'the lashings of caviar, the grand air of luxury, nothing left out but cleanliness.' An American pesticide took care of the bedbugs that gnawed the Prime Minister's feet on the first night.' (Wernick, 2011, 12).

Stalin took advantage of the late hour set for the summit on February 4th to meet separately with Churchill and Roosevelt prior to the actual conference. To Churchill, he suggested the British plan of a major offensive into the Ruhr industrial region and another towards Vienna, ideas favored by the English but eschewed by the Americans, who preferred a massive onslaught all along Germany's Western frontier.

Somehow, Churchill failed to draw the obvious inference from this proposal. Stalin suggested a strategic plan identical to Britain's top secret military schemes, yet the Prime Minister did not make the connection that Soviet spies must be active in the British government, leaking highly classified information to the Eastern ally for whom Churchill already entertained a deep distrust.

When speaking with Roosevelt, Stalin switched tactics, urging a massive advance along the whole Western front. Again, Roosevelt, perhaps taken in by Stalin's personable manner, overlooked the Soviet leader's intimate knowledge of plans he should not possess. Stalin thus ensured both men felt well-disposed towards him at the start.

In fact, the Soviet NKGB military intelligence spies in London had acquired a complete copy of the detailed British memorandum on negotiating goals and strategy for Yalta. The Soviets provided a translated copy of this document to Stalin, who memorized much of its content before Roosevelt and Churchill even arrived. In effect, he already had full insight into every detail of the Western Allies' negotiating plans and even their disagreements, while his own purposes remained totally opaque to the other men.

As soon as the Big Three gathered at 5 PM, Stalin again showcased his diplomatic dexterity. He proposed Roosevelt should speak first and act as the arbitrator during the discussion. Through this simple device, which pleased the American president immensely, he subtly divided the British and American leaders by making the latter the "referee" who needed to judge their British ally as well as the Russians, while simultaneously putting the weaker partner in the role of chief negotiator with the Soviets. Charles Bohlen, Roosevelt's interpreter, noted the slapdash methods of the summit with dismay, though he also pointed out the one advantage of this chaos: "The conference [...] was organized in such a way that there was no orderly discussion and resolution of each problem by the leaders. Instead, issues were brought up, discussed, then shunted off to the Foreign Ministers or military chiefs or just dropped for a few hours. [...] It is a wonder that any agreements could emerge from such confusion. But the constant switch from one subject to another kept tempers cool." (Bohlen, 1973, 179).

Bohlen

The agenda for the first day's discussion consisted mostly of military affairs. The Soviets gave the Western Allies the first detailed briefing on the Eastern front situation and their immediate offensive plans. General of the Army Aleksei Antonov, speaking through Stalin's personal interpreter Vladimir Pavlov, provided the report. He outlined the powerful Soviet winter offensive that drove simultaneous thrusts through Poland, Hungary, and East Prussia, astounding the Westerners with the scope and success of the Soviet advance.

Antonov

Roosevelt, showing that his mind remained active under the mask of illness that sometimes made him appear almost catatonic, asked a surprisingly penetrating question. He interrupted Antonov, asking whether the Russians had converted the railways in Eastern Europe from European gauge to the broader Soviet gauge in order to bring up their supplies. The question represented more than idle curiosity; if the Soviets had rebuilt the railways to match their own gauge, then permanent occupation seemed more likely. Antonov, put on the spot, replied that the Soviets had indeed replaced the European gauge railway with their own. This tacit admission of conquest, rather than liberation, drew another shrewd remark from the American president: "As our armies are now approaching each other in Germany it was important that the staffs should discuss this problem so that there would be a definite place in Germany where the different gauges would meet." (Mee, 2014, 9).

Stalin himself took over from Antonov at this point, no doubt to the general's relief. The Soviet dictator, perhaps taken aback himself by the diplomatic but penetrating statement, assured Roosevelt that most of Germany's railroads would continue to use standard European gauge, a roundabout assurance against unlimited westward advance.

After the meeting, Churchill wanted to confer with Roosevelt privately. However, the American president refused, not wanting the Soviets to think the Westerners underhanded. Roosevelt persisted in this isolation for approximately the first half of the conference, causing mounting desperation among the English and even his own staff. Presidential adviser Harry Hopkins, later unjustly defamed as a traitor based on bizarrely flimsy "evidence," flew into a rage and attempted to enter Roosevelt's quarters to persuade him to work in concert with Churchill. However, Anna Roosevelt Boettiger calmly turned him away, repeating FDR's formula that nothing should be done to upset the Soviets or make them suspicious.

Roosevelt's determination not to "gang up" on Stalin ensured the divide between the British and Americans continued into the second day of the summit. The Big Three met for dinner, enjoying a friendly meal despite the confusions and differences already arising. Stalin, swallowing his hatred for Churchill, proposed a toast to the short, crumpled, bulldog figure sitting near him at the laden table: "It was due, said Stalin, 'in large measure to Mr. Churchill's courage and staunchness, [that] England, when she stood alone, had divided the might of Hitlerite Germany at a time when the rest of Europe was falling flat on its face before Hitler,' and Great Britain, 'had carried on the fight alone.' In all history, said Stalin, there were few examples 'where the courage of one man had been so important to the future history of the world.'" (Mee, 2014, 7-8).

Charles Bohlen, Roosevelt's translator and one of his advisers, took one of the menus and managed to convince the Big Three to sign it as a souvenir. His action preserved for history the exact food items on offer, including expected dishes such as caviar, red and white salmon, cream of chicken, Swiss cheese, roast partridge, ice cream, and roasted almonds, but also more exotic dishes like sturgeon in aspic, sucking [*sic*] pig in horseradish sauce, and "wild goat of the steppes."

Churchill and Stalin

The dinner conversation naturally turned to the topic of the summit itself, and the United Nations. Stalin said that the larger powers (the USSR, USA, and British Empire) should essentially govern the postwar world, and the small nations be permitted to offer their opinions but not interfere with the plans of the major countries. Churchill, for once, agreed with the Soviet strongman at least in spirit, famously stating, "The eagle should let the small birds sing and care not wherefore they sang." This statement paraphrased part of a speech delivered in William Shakespeare's *Titus Andronicus*. Roosevelt, however, still preferred the notion of all the "birds" having an equal voice in decision-making, the system actually adopted.

While the Big Three talked, Soviet Deputy Foreign Minister Andrei Vyshinsky engaged in a rather sharp-edged exchange with Charles Bohlen: "When the leaders began discussing the right of dissent within countries, Vishinsky turned to me and said that he thought that the American people should learn to obey their leaders and not question what they were told to do. I replied with some sarcasm that I would like to see him go to the United States and tell that to the American people. With a grin, Vishinsky said that he would be glad to do so." (Bohlen, 1973,).

Cracks appeared in the British delegation as a loud argument erupted between Churchill and Sir Anthony Eden after dinner. Churchill maintained that the Big Three plus China should be the main arbiters of the United Nations, while Eden, favoring votes for all countries, threatened to bring the matter before Parliament.

Before the start of talks on February 5th, Roosevelt ate lunch with Harry Hopkins, a leisurely meal enabling 90 minutes of discussion between the two Americans. Hopkins briefed the president on the details of the agenda, and also presented a plan for detaching the Ruhr and Saar industrial regions from Germany for direct Allied administration, while leaving the rest of the nation largely intact. Roosevelt expressed his liking for this scheme.

Roosevelt took the initiative at the start of the second day's meeting, which began at 4:15 PM. The American president attempted to set the agenda by saying that he wanted to use the session to decide on zones of occupation in Germany. He also proposed including a French zone, handing Stalin a map prepared by his staff showing a possible division of German territory between the U.S., British, French, and Soviets.

After Roosevelt's surprising acumen the day before in the discussion of Soviet railway modifications, Stalin seemed determined to regain the dominant position in the talks. Rather than responding to FDR's map and statement, he ignored both and instead peppered the other two men with a list of items he wanted to discuss: reparations payments from the Germans to the Allies, the form of government in conquered Germany, the precise meaning of "unconditional surrender," and the matter of dismembering the German state, which Roosevelt raised previously at Tehran.

Roosevelt tried to regain control of the negotiations by suggesting these items could be folded into his larger discussion about occupation zones. Stalin pushed inexorably, however, calling German dismemberment the most pressing issue. The Soviet dictator threw the earlier words of the Western leaders back in their teeth, reminding them that Churchill had suggested a 3-way dismemberment of Germany during his Moscow visit, and that Roosevelt had proposed five separate countries at Tehran. Thus, Stalin adroitly placed his two opponents (as they, in fact, were from the Soviet perspective) on the defensive. He pushed his advantage by bringing out charts prepared by Maxim Litvinov and his staff, illustrating 4-way, 5-way, and 7-way divisions of Germany into small, feeble nations. The Soviet Union, of course, preferred an enfeebled German state, unable to threaten Stalin's Eastern European conquests and presenting a trivial barrier to future expansionism against the hated capitalist republics.

Finally, after a few moments of discomfiture, Churchill responded to Stalin's bombshell with a method that proved the main outcome of the Yalta Conference on almost all matters: deferment to some unspecified future time. He stated, " In principle all were agreed on the dismemberment of Germany, but the actual method was much too complicated to settle here in five or six days. It would require a very searching examination of the historical, ethnographical and economic facts and would need prolonged consideration by a special committee, which would have to go into the different proposals put forward and advise on them." (Plokhy, 2010, 115).

Faced with a question too prickly to resolve immediately – especially since the Prime Minister had severe, independent doubts about dismembering Germany with a menacing Soviet Union looming on the European horizon – Churchill tried to shunt the question away. Stalin, however, declined to let the two Westerners off the hook so easily. When the talk shifted to unconditional surrender, the Soviet leader proposed that one of the central items in the surrender should be a recognition of dismemberment as inevitable, with only its precise form remaining in doubt. Churchill, driven to desperation, point-blank refused. At this point, Roosevelt stepped in his role as "umpire" between the English and Soviet leaders. He agreed with Stalin to some degree at least, but then launched into an incoherent speech which alarmed Charles Bohlen, who for the first time considered that the FDR's illness might be severely affecting his mental state: "The President rambled on about the Germany he had known in 1886, when small, semi-autonomous states such as Darmstadt and Rothenburg thrived. The centralization of Germany in the Berlin government was one of the causes, he said, of the ills from which the world was suffering. Roosevelt's rambling and inconclusive statement, which didn't even hang together, was greeted with polite indifference by the Soviet leaders and by slight signs of boredom by the British." (Bohlen, 1973, 183).

The discussion went on following Roosevelt's peculiar interruption, but Churchill's viewpoint gradually won out. The Big Three agreed to place the matter before a committee consisting of the U.S. and Soviet ambassadors to Britain, plus Sir Anthony Eden, the British Foreign Secretary. This committee never actually formed, and thus the postponement of a decision about German dismemberment became, de facto, a complete abandonment of the idea.

With the decision to leave the matter of dismemberment undecided reached, the negotiators moved to another topic. Roosevelt returned to the question of giving the French an occupation zone in Germany, a concept he supported. However, he almost immediately left himself open for correction by Stalin by saying the French did not want Germany territory up to the Rhine, when in fact Charles de Gaulle had stated exactly that while speaking with Stalin in Moscow the previous year. The three men fenced verbally over the French question. Stalin opposed it, Roosevelt favored it, and Churchill attempted to mediate by suggesting the French occupation zone be created from portions of the American and English occupation zones, thus leaving the Soviets in control of the same amount of territory as they would have enjoyed without the French being admitted.

Stalin, who loathed the French for their rapid surrender to the Germans and their president Charles de Gaulle because his prickly nature irritated the Soviet leader, continued to object. Roosevelt finally suggested that the French be given an occupation zone but no seat on the "control commission" governing Germany, and that final details should be postponed to be worked out "later." As so often happened, the decision was to take no decision at all. Both Churchill and Stalin reluctantly agreed to this formula, which promised a French role but deliberately avoided defining it.

With the first two items disposed of in this fashion, Stalin ordered the translator and Deputy People's Commissar for Foreign Affairs, Ivan Maisky, to present the Soviet demands for German reparations. Maisky, already enmeshed in the brutal toils of Soviet politics and on his way to an arrest from which he only just escaped with his life due to his earlier Menshovik leanings, responded with alarm to the hostile dictator's one-word command to him: "Report!" Nevertheless, Maisky had prepared thoroughly and laid out the Soviet reparations scheme with clarity and detail. Reparations, in fact, had one of the highest priorities in Stalin's thinking. The Soviet premier wanted a fixed sum of reparations named at the conference, and the issue would reappear time and again at Yalta, in addition to the subsequent Potsdam Conference.

Maisky (right)

Maisky laid out a plan breathtaking in its scope. The Soviets envisioned not only stripping Germany of all its industry, but also deporting millions of German men and women to the Soviet

Union as forced labor. This suggestion amounted to the idea of enslaving a sizable chunk of the German population in lieu of cash payments from the prostrate Reich, a notion that would not have been out of place in the warfare of ancient Rome or the Assyrian or Mongolian empires.

Maisky asked Stalin for permission to speak directly to the other two leaders in English, which the Soviet leader assented to. Maisky knew the Westerners well enough to downplay the issue of mass enslavement; he judged this, probably correctly, to be political dynamite capable of uniting Churchill and Roosevelt against Stalin. Instead, he adroitly stated the Soviets wanted $10 billion in reparations, some of which might be exacted as "labor," an element he deliberately left vague.

Churchill, pointing out that Germany had barely managed to pay £1 billion after World War I, and with most of the money supplied by the United States at that, shot back, "If you want a horse to pull your wagon, you have to give him some hay." Stalin, intervening, engaged in a back and forth exchange of aggressive metaphors until Roosevelt interrupted. The American president again largely took Stalin's side, against the advice of both Harry Hopkins and Charles Bohlen. The wrangling continued until the Big Three agreed to another postponement, this one to allow a "Reparations Commission" to determine the exact size and nature of the reparations payments. As with the other committees, commissions, and boards spawned by Yalta, this one accomplished precisely nothing. The issue reached a settlement at Potsdam, with the shrewd, pragmatic, suspicious Harry S. Truman as the main U.S. negotiator.

Temporarily exhausted by the stormy, inconclusive wrangling, the Big Three dined together again late on February 5th. That night, Stalin held a council at the Soviet headquarters in the Yusupov Palace with his advisers. Concerned he had pushed too hard, the Russian strongman finally settled on a new sum of $7 billion in reparations to the Soviet Union and $8 billion divided among the Western Allies.

Roosevelt awakened on the morning of February 6th with the intention of turning the discussion to the matter of the United Nations. Churchill, meanwhile, rose in a gloomy mood, speaking to his personal doctor of the likelihood of future war with the Soviet Union.

Due to the deliberations the previous day, several of the Big Three's lieutenants – the American Stettinius, an inveterate and fanatical supporter of Roosevelt, the British Sir Anthony Eden, and Molotov – convened at Livadia Palace. These three men comprised the "Dismemberment Committee" chosen the day before during the turbulent plenary session. Since most of the world now appeared aware that the three top Allied leaders had met for some purpose, the Committee first decided to prepare a communique for their chiefs' later approval. The Third Reich, in particular, attempted to sow dissension by spreading many rumors and canards about the meeting by radio, which prompted Stettinius, Eden, and Molotov to respond more soberly.

Their communique stated that the Big Three and their chiefs of staff attended a summit near the Black Sea (without divulging the exact location) and went on to describe their overall agenda: "Their purpose is to concert plans for completing the defeat of the common enemy and for building, with their Allies, firm foundations for a lasting peace. [...] The conference began with military discussions. The present situation on all the European fronts has been reviewed and the fullest information interchanged. [...] Discussions of problems involved in establishing a secure peace have also begun. These discussions will cover joint plans for the occupation and control of Germany [...] A communiqué will be issued at the conclusion of the Conference." (Stettinius, 1949, 135-136).

The three men discussed the dismemberment of Germany and, like their leaders the day before, soon decided it represented too complex a matter to decide on short notice. The entire result of the Dismemberment Committee's meeting consisted of the decision to hand off responsibility for the decision to the European Advisory Commission, continuing the black comedy of "passing the buck" initiated by the Big Three themselves. Before adjourning for a friendly lunch in the Palace sunroom – which offered a spectacular view over the Black Sea – the trio agreed that a recommendation be passed to the European Advisory Commission for inclusion of the word "dismemberment" in the EAC's main statement. They could not agree on the phrasing, however, and the final wording used by the EAC bore little resemblance to any of their suggestions.

Stalin, Roosevelt, and Churchill met again in the Great Hall at 4 PM, enjoying the warmth of a huge log fire built in one of the palace's capacious hearths. Stalin, unlike his behavior on previous days, smoked one cigarette after another, possibly indicating irritation or nervousness.

The Dismemberment Committee first reported their non-decision to their superiors and obtained the Big Three's approval for the communique announcing the summit to the world. Roosevelt then presented his plan for the United Nations, an updated and revamped version of the failed League of Nations established at the end of World War I. He provided a general outline of the concept and predicted its creation would ensure fifty years of peace in the world.

Stettinius then delivered a backup presentation describing the functions of the Security Council. Perhaps recalling the dinner discussion during which both Churchill and Stalin expressed reservations about allowing the smaller countries full voting privileges, he stressed the importance and power and of the Security Council within the UN, along with the fact that the US, USSR, and UK would be permanent members of that body. The Security Council would consist of seven representatives in all.

Due to translation difficulties and natural paranoia, the Soviets initially believed that the Western Allies sought to trick them with the Security Council and voting arrangements. With some effort, Charles Bohlen managed to provide a more satisfactory explanation of the setup. Stalin and Molotov, however, requested that the Americans prepare a detailed written explanation for presentation during the February 7th plenary session.

Churchill affirmed his support for the overall scheme, but now took the line that the Great Powers should create a grievance system to ensure fair treatment of the smaller or weaker countries. This intervention by Churchill triggered an aggressive response from Stalin. Using biting sarcasm, the Soviet leader attacked the British Prime Minister's assertion that this measure might prevent the Great Powers being seen as trying to rule the world. Though Roosevelt and Stettinius tried to calm the situation, Stalin burst forth in a tirade that shattered the momentary appearance of unanimity. The Soviet leader declared that an alliance between the Great Powers represented the sole guarantor of peace, while the involvement of smaller nations would muddy this all-important issue. Then, eerily, the Soviet strongman turned to the two Western statesmen and uttered words almost quoted verbatim from Churchill's statements to his doctor that morning during his private breakfast. This startlingly precise echo of the Prime Minister's statement almost certainly points to Soviet listening devices throughout the quarters of both visiting Western groups: "They all knew that as long as the three of them lived none of them would involve their countries in aggressive actions, but after all, ten years from now none of them might be present. A new generation would come into the present not knowing the horrors of the present war." (Plokhy, 2010, 141). The statement clearly harkened back to Churchill's earlier fear of inevitable war with Russia.

Finally, Roosevelt broke in to state that no member of the Security Council could be evicted without the unanimous agreement of all the others. Stalin, though he stopped his tirade, stated that he expected to resume the topic of the UN the following day, when he had more complete information at his disposal.

With the matter of the United Nations addressed to the extent the ad hoc conditions of the summit allowed, another controversial topic arose – the matter of postwar Poland. Churchill proved desperately anxious to ensure a democratic government in Poland, since the entire war began in an effort to rescue the Poles from conquest and tyrannical foreign domination. However, he had no way to coerce the Soviets into leaving the country after having taken it, short of deploying armed force, and all three of the men and their advisers tacitly understood this fact.

Stalin's plan was to keep all Polish territory east of the Curzon Line, effectively that portion first obtained by the Soviet Union during its period of alliance with Nazi Germany, and remove a slice of Eastern Germany to fill out Polish territory in the west in "compensation." In arguing his point, the Soviet leader showed all his considerable skills to greatest advantage, though of course he also possessed an unassailable position. Stalin quite clearly intended to keep Poland as province of the Soviet empire, and in particular viewed his nation's seizure of Poland's Eastern extremities as permanent, even though made in concert with the now-hated Third Reich.

Roosevelt, on the other hand, wanted free elections (as did Churchill) and asked Stalin to release the Polish-majority city of Lvov and the economically critical oil fields of Drohobych nearby to Poland. The American president also suggested forming five political parties in Poland, one of which would be communist. During this speech, supported by Churchill's statements, Stalin grew more and more excited. Finally, he rose to his feet and began to outline his rebuttal: "A sure clue to the gravity of the problem was Stalin's getting up and walking up and down behind his chair while expounding his points. His best debating skill stood out on the Polish question. When Roosevelt said he wanted the Polish election to be pure, like Caesar's wife, Stalin commented, 'They said that about her but in fact she had her sins.'" (Bohlen, 1973, 187).

Though Stalin stated he wanted a "strong, democratic" Poland in an effort to mollify the Westerners, he also emphatically refused to modify the Curzon Line boundary or hand back Lvov. He shrugged off Western appeals to honor and fairness by forcefully invoking security and the life-or-death nature of Russia's need to block Germany's "invasion corridor" into Soviet territory. The rest of the session consisted of Stalin stonewalling Roosevelt's and Churchill's efforts to secure a free Poland.

Roosevelt could not abandon the matter, however. Even after the leaders retired to their respective palaces, he wrote a long letter to Stalin, appealing to the Soviet strongman on the grounds that Polish-American voters would be displeased by the failure to secure an independent Poland. The president's advisers judged this argument unlikely to move the dictator – and, perhaps, calculated to persuade him of FDR's weakness – but nevertheless did their duty by delivering it to the Soviets.

On February 7th, Stettinius, Eden, and Molotov met again prior to the main plenary session at 4 PM. Harry Hopkins and James Byrnes asked Stettinius to focus on the United Nations Security Council question during his consultation with Molotov, rather than Poland, due to their concern with avoiding the complete collapse of the UN idea. However, the three men first discussed the question of dismemberment (again referring it to an EAC decision) and reparations. The Soviets returned to their initial figure of $10 billion in payments to the Soviet Union and an equal amount to the Western Allies. The discussion of the reparations, and the possibility of a Moscow-based Reparations Commission, occupied all of the time remaining until the plenary session, meaning the three foreign ministers failed to discuss Poland in detail on the 7th despite Hopkins' and Byrnes' urging.

Roosevelt raised the Polish issue immediately when the Big Three met that afternoon, suggesting that representatives of both the Soviet puppet "Lublin Government" and the Polish government in exile in London be invited to Yalta to participate fully in the summit. Stalin deflected the question by saying that he could not yet contact the Lublin Poles, and that his staff continued preparing an answer to Roosevelt's letter of the evening before.

The Soviets then abruptly announced that they fully accepted the Security Council voting process for the United Nations. Briefly, the Americans and to a lesser degree the British basked in the pure happiness of seeing the UN proposal rescued from what they believed would be certain rejection. However, Molotov continued his presentation and stated flatly that the Soviet Union need two, or possibly three, additional seats in the UN to represent the most important of its 16 republics.

The Americans balked, knowing the republics had no independence whatsoever from the dictatorship in Moscow. The measure simply granted the Soviet Union extra seats and votes. Roosevelt, nonplussed, scribbled a handwritten note saying "This is not so good" and gave it to Stettinius. Molotov elaborated that Belarus, Lithuania, and the Ukraine (where fierce fighting continued between Ukrainian separatists and Soviet NKVD enforcers) would ideally comprise the additional UN member states. Roosevelt recovered fast, however, and responded with the inevitable technique used throughout the Yalta Conference – a postponement. He suggested that a commission meet in March to iron out the details of the United Nations and create a charter. The UN itself would likely not form until approximately half a year after the charter's acceptance.

The talk turned briefly to Iran, then back to the vexed question of Poland. Molotov laid out a proposal that moved the Curzon Line approximately 3 miles eastward, granted Poland a piece of Germany up to the Rivers Oder and Neisse, and admitted a handful of London Poles to the "Polish Provisional Government" (that is, Stalin's puppet Lublin regime). Churchill continued to argue for some time, but it quickly became clear that Stalin would do what he wished with Poland in any case.

After the plenary session, Roosevelt and Stettinius conferred about Stalin's demand for extra USSR seats in the UN General Assembly. Roosevelt decided that two additional members represented an acceptable compromise, since India – entirely a British Empire possession at the time – had a seat also. FDR selected Belarus and the Ukraine as these members, remarking that the most important task at the moment consisted of keeping the three major Allied states united to defeat Germany.

The three foreign secretaries met at the British lodgings on February 8th, with Sir Anthony Eden serving as host. They first discussed the matter of Iranian oil, which American companies expressed an interest in purchasing. Stettinius wanted a date by which the Soviets would withdraw their soldiers from Iran, but Molotov stalled, saying that the question needed more investigation. They also chose April 25th for the first meeting in the United States for creation of the UN charter, pushing back the schedule from Roosevelt's extremely quick March date.

By this time, Roosevelt started showing signs of exhaustion – the summit continued to wear him out, lowering his ability to muster the energy to argue against the other two men's positions. FDR and Stalin met for a short talk before the start of the 5th plenary session, during which the president informed the Soviet premier that he was amenable to the addition of two more Soviet client states to the UN.

Roosevelt and Eden opened the session with the announcement that two more Soviet "republics" would join the UN. This declaration stunned many of the other participants; even Alger Hiss had argued vehemently against allowing the Soviets more than a single vote in the United Nations. Stalin, however, remained dissatisfied, querying why so many countries that never declared war on Germany should be included in the UN. With the adroitness of a career politician, FDR shifted the blame for this to Sumner Welles, previous Secretary of State and conveniently absent from Yalta.

The other Americans revolted so powerfully against the USSR receiving three votes that Roosevelt agreed to ask the American people if they wanted three. In the event, the American press and electorate met the idea with mockery, and the United States contented itself with a single vote.

With this arrangement in place, the discussion turned again to a wrangle over Poland. Churchill argued at length that the 150,000 Polish soldiers fighting alongside the Commonwealth troops had little liking for the Lublin government, and that their voices deserved to be heard in a general election also. Stalin shot back that the Soviet Union had not objected when the Western Allies placed unelected official Charles de Gaulle at the head of liberated France without consulting with their Eastern ally first: "Neither had been elected, and he could not say which one enjoyed the greatest degree of popularity—yet we all had dealt with de Gaulle and the Soviet Government concluded a treaty with him. Why should we be so different with regard to the Polish Government, and why could we not deal with an enlarged Polish Government?" (Plokhy, 2010, 212-213).

Roosevelt agreed to drop the topic for the time being once Stalin assured him elections would occur in Poland within a month – if possible. Stalin also laid out his plans for shifting Poland's borders westward, assuring the Allies that large numbers of ethnic Germans in Poland would not present a problem because most of the people fled before the raping, slaughtering advance of the Red Army (though he merely reported the flight of millions westward and omitted mention of the numerous Soviet war crimes). In fact, the Soviets already formed those who failed to flee into "work battalions" to provide slave labor for the Soviet conquerors, and to strip the new Polish territory of any remaining Teutonic population. However, this matter did not appear in the discussions. Instead, the Soviets brought up the matter of allowing Marshal Tito to create an interim government in Yugoslavia, while Churchill thanked Stalin for not interfering in British interests in Greece.

Tito

Military matters followed on the day's agenda after the long talk over Poland subsided. Roosevelt requested that the Soviets allow American bombers to land at advance Russian airfields and for the Soviets to allow teams of Western experts to examine bomb damage behind Soviet lines, both of which the communist premier agreed to. Additionally, Roosevelt pushed for Soviet intervention in the war against Japan. At this stage, it remained unclear if an atomic weapon could ever be developed, and Admiral Leahy thought the nuclear bomb would remain a pipe dream. Stalin agreed to help against Japan, though he significantly set no time parameters for Russian intervention. He also wanted the Kurile Islands for the Soviet Union. With Russia's aid against Japan apparently secured, Roosevelt thought that he had made real progress despite the continuing problems over Poland.

The day ended with a spectacular and extremely cordial dinner at the Yusupov Palace. The meal consisted of 25 courses, while the diners drank no less than 45 toasts. The dining continued until midnight. Perhaps mellowed by the freely flowing liquor, Churchill abandoned his pessimistic attitude and spoke of an optimistic future in which peace and prosperity might flourish for all.

The three foreign ministers carried out their usual meeting prior to the plenary session on February 9th. Stettinius and Eden pushed for a Soviet commitment regarding free elections in Poland, unwilling to abandon the Eastern European nation despite the fact it already represented a prize of war for the Red Army. Molotov responded evasively, promising elections in the near future but pointing out that the Russians could not risk a hostile Poland in their rear if an anti-Soviet government took office.

Stettinius, distrusting the Soviets strongly, pressed the matter, asking for a completely new, elected government to replace the Soviet-appointed Lublin state entirely. Molotov, keeping his calm, stated in reply that Polish exiles would find places in the government, but that the Lublin bureaucrats would continue administering the Polish nation until further notice. Meanwhile, the Russian agreed to some largely meaningless, but appropriate-sounding, changes to the official tripartite announcements about Poland.

The three men then moved to the question of reparations, again engaging in largely circular arguments that failed to clarify the vague "agreements" already reached.

The sixth plenary session opened with a report from the three ministers, followed by an intermission. A rather pointed exchange then arose over Yugoslavia. Churchill openly asked if Stalin earmarked Marshal Tito as the nation's dictator, while demanding immediate elections. The Soviet strongman dodged the question of dictatorship, stating he wanted Tito to form a "stable government" after which elections would occur when the situation seemed appropriate. Stalin agreed to allow observers at the eventual Yugoslav elections, while he remained more evasive regarding Polish electoral matters. Churchill, in turn, invited Soviet observers to the polls in Greece.

With almost nothing concretely decided beyond plans to begin the United Nations, the Big Three turned their attention to drafting a sonorous, ringing "Declaration on Liberated Europe." Here, the three leaders found themselves in near agreement, since the Declaration confined itself mostly to generalities rather than specific, actionable plans.

Churchill insisted on the inclusion of a sentence noting that the British Empire already complied with the Atlantic Charter (guaranteeing the self-determination of countries), and that the elements of the British Empire therefore gained no right to dissolve it based on the Declaration. The Prime Minister thus made a final bid to preserve his nation as a global superpower despite the emergence of the U.S. and USSR.

The session touched briefly on war criminals. Churchill initially suggested drawing up a list at Yalta and simply shooting these Germans immediately when captured. However, he almost immediately reversed his position, arguing for the postponement of the list's creation and for full judicial proceedings to ensure a fair trial for the defendants. Neither Roosevelt nor Stalin objected to these provisions.

The sixth day's negotiations ended with a short report on the Western Front situation, followed by dinner. Molotov, Eden, and Stettinius met again following the repast to try to address the Polish question. Once again, the negotiations proved largely fruitless. The Soviet agreed to suggest the creation of a new government called the Polish Provisional Government of National Unity at the next day's plenary session, but details remained scarce.

With very little time remaining in the brief Yalta Conference, Stettinius and Roosevelt met on the morning of February 10th, 1945 to plan strategy for the day. They discussed Poland as one of the main outstanding problems yet to be resolved. The two men decided to withdraw some language Stalin found objectionable, but in exchange they expected to be allowed to observe elections not only in Yugoslavia but also Poland: "'If we agree to withdraw this sentence,' President Roosevelt said, 'it must clearly be understood that we fully expect our ambassador to observe and report on the elections. If the statement of this fact in the agreement irritates the Russians, we can drop the statement, but they must understand our firm determination that the ambassadors will observe and report on the elections in any case." (Stettinius, 1949, 252).

Molotov, Eden, and Stettinius then fine-tuned the phrasing of the Declaration on Liberated Europe. They also briefly touched again on reparations, Iran, Yugoslavia, and the other conference topics, but they could not work out any additional agreements on any of the topics. The plenary meeting then occurred in the Great Hall, with Roosevelt, as usual, sitting closest to the roaring log fire in deference to his illness.

While the meeting spent much of its time polishing and reconfiguring the Declaration, Stalin and Churchill began a passionate argument about reparations. Stalin insisted on naming a specific dollar figure of $20 billion total, half for the Soviets, while Churchill, with equal stubbornness, maintained no amount should be designated. Finally, the Prime Minister and the Soviet Premier agreed to instruct the Moscow Commission to determine the exact amount of reparations. Roosevelt stated, "The answer is simple; Judge Roosevelt approves and the document is accepted." (Buhite, 1986, 36).

Stalin also raised the matter of the Turks' right to close the Dardanelles if they felt war imminent, thus blocking Russia's Mediterranean access from the Black Sea. Churchill agreed to speak with the Turkish government to modernize the arrangement, giving the Soviet Union greater access.

With their meeting drawing to a close, the three men relaxed somewhat and joked together about one another's actions and statements. A final discussion of Poland's fate occurred, with the Western frontier remaining fluid and undefined for the time being due to Roosevelt's inability to set boundaries during negotiations.

With departures planned for the 11th, the Big Three handed the list of decisions, such as they were, over to a drafting committee with orders to prepare a communique. In the meantime, a select group of men went for cocktails and dinner, including Stalin, Roosevelt, Churchill, Stettinius, Bohlen, Churchill's interpreter Major Arthur Birse, Eden, Molotov, and Pavlov.

The Soviet chefs had outdone themselves with a gourmet meal. The men drank toasts to each other, to absent friends, and to success in the war and a peaceful future afterward. Churchill and Stalin both tried to persuade Roosevelt to remain for a few more days, but the American president remained firm – he would leave at 3 PM on the 11th to meet several Middle Eastern kings and try to negotiate regarding Palestine.

On the following morning, February 11th, 1945, the Big Three met to approve the text of the Declaration and the communique. Wilder Foote, Stettinius' assistant, prepared the documents. Churchill suggested a grammatical change to remove the word "joint," which he said reminded him of mutton, but the documents otherwise stood mostly as Foote had drafted them. Roosevelt and Churchill both said "Horosho," the Russian word for "good," while Stalin assented with an English "Okay."

The three men signed the Declaration in alphabetical order, Churchill first, then Roosevelt, and finally Stalin, an arrangement that coincidentally also placed the leaders in order of age, oldest to youngest. Stalin wanted to be last to avoid the imputation by the foreign press that he had coerced the other two into signing the document. The Big Three ate lunch together, drank a glass of brandy, and parted with handshakes, compliments, and gifts. Roosevelt, who would die within a few months, would not see the other two leaders again.

Sarah Oliver, Churchill's daughter, described how quickly Yalta assumed an abandoned appearance again in one of her letters: "Stalin, like some genie, just disappeared. Three hours after the last handshake, Yalta was deserted, except for those who always have to tidy up after the party." (Plokhy, 2010, 328). In fact, most of the staff members of the three entourages remained for most of the day, working out the final details, signing documents, and forwarding the information to their respective governments. With their leaders gone, the men attempted to persuade each other to accept changes to the documents they thought appropriate. Sir Anthony Eden, for example, tried to add Saudi Arabia to the list of UN members on the grounds that it would be "good to have a Moslem or two," but Molotov refused. The departing men took branches of the lemon tree as souvenirs, stripping the unfortunate plant totally.

With Roosevelt gone, Churchill found himself abandoned by Stalin, who no longer felt the need to show cordiality to the Englishman now that his powerful American ally had left. The Prime Minister moped about for a few hours, then exploded into a frenzy of energy, ordering his staff to pack and leaving Yalta at 5 PM in his official car. Churchill arrived in Sevastopol two hours later and immediately boarded the HMS *Franconia*, calling loudly and cheerfully for a dinner of English food without the Russians' "cold fatty approaches to all their meals."

The bulldog-like Prime Minister, bursting with good spirits, exclaimed that he was glad the "bloody" conference was finished. His joy at escaping Yalta and the endless wrangling of the conference prompted him to sing the British song "Soldiers of the Queen:"

"It's the Soldiers of the Queen, my lads

Who've been my lads,

Who're seen my lads,

In the fight for England's glory, lads,

When we've had to show them what we mean:

And when we say we've always won,

And when they ask us how it's done,

We'll proudly point to ev'ry one

of England's soldiers of the Queen!"

Like his British counterpart, Roosevelt dined eagerly on home fare, Texas steak, aboard the USS *Catoctin* the night he left, but the president was exhausted after the Yalta Conference. Many, including FDR himself, thought the lull in the war allowed the stress of the previous years to finally catch up with him. Shortly after he returned home, Roosevelt went to the spas of Warm Springs, Georgia, where he had spent much time attempting to recover from paralysis after attracting polio. While sitting for a presidential portrait painting, Roosevelt complained of sudden headaches. Hours later, on April 12th, 1945, still sitting for the portrait, Roosevelt slumped forward and died of a massive stroke, less than a month before victory would be achieved in Europe.

Roosevelt's death was met with shock in the U.S. and around the world. Though his health had been declining, and he seemed out of it at times at Yalta, the public knew little about his illness. He was 63 at the time of death. Churchill did not attend the funeral. He may well have been too busy to cross the Atlantic, but critics have suggested that there was an element of sour grapes in the decision.

Chapter 5: The Declaration and Other Documents

The Declaration on Liberated Europe and other documents published at the end of the Yalta Conference, the fruits of Operation Argonaut, consisted mostly of what Stalin called "algebra" – fancy but relatively meaningless verbiage – rather than "arithmetic" – practical, actionable plans. The Declaration included nine sections:

1.   The Defeat of Germany. This section essentially stated that the three major Allies would continue fighting Germany until they won.

2.   The Occupation and Control of Germany. Section 2 started with a statement of the decision to demand unconditional surrender. From there it went on to note the creation of four occupation zones for the Americans, British, Soviets, and French, but naturally gave no indications of the exact boundaries involved.

3.   Reparation by Germany. This section simply stated the Allies would extract an unspecified war reparation from the defeated Reich.

4.   United Nations Conference. The Big Three noted their intention to found the United Nations as soon as possible, with a conference on the subject scheduled for San Francisco, California on April 25th.

5.   Declaration of Liberated Europe. This section gave lengthy but very general descriptions of how the Allies would restore the right to self-determination to Europe's nations, in accordance with the Atlantic Charter.

6.   Poland. The sixth item stated that the Polish Provisional Government of National Unity would be formed via free elections but did not specify when these would occur.

7.   Yugoslavia. The Big Three agreed Marshal Tito would create a government in Yugoslavia, on an allegedly temporary basis but with no indication when a democratic government would be established.

8.   Meetings of Foreign Secretaries. This section suggested Stettinius, Eden, and Molotov might continue meeting every quarter to continue friendly coordination between their governments.

9.   Unity for Peace as for War. The three leaders pledged to cooperate in peacetime as well as during the remainder of World War II.

Another document consisted of the Protocol of the Proceedings of the Crimea Conference, which went into more detail (such as the $20 billion reparation amount) but left the final decision on almost everything to future, ill-defined committees or conferences. The most concrete section described the membership and voting procedures of the United Nations, the part of the negotiations the Big Three agreed on most clearly.

The final, short agreement called for the entry of the Soviet Union into the Pacific War, but it left the timing entirely up to Stalin and offered him the Kurile Islands in exchange. In the event, the Soviets finally attacked the Japanese only on the eve of their surrender, seizing the ill-defended puppet state of Manchukuo and illegally continuing the assault on the Japanese after their surrender in order to acquire additional territory.

Chapter 6: The Yalta Conference's Results

The outcome of the Yalta Conference remains highly controversial in interpretations of World War II. Some praise the Western Allies for winning more than they might otherwise have through adroit negotiation with the aggressive Soviet state. Others condemn Roosevelt as either a naïve fool or even a sort of quisling, failing to counter Stalin's demands and thus abandoning Eastern Europe to its fate as the footstool of the relentless Stalinist empire.

In fact, though evidence can be combed from the records to support multiple viewpoints, the most plausible explanation remains that the Yalta Conference proved largely futile mostly because little room for discussion existed. Stalin already held most the territory his country would retain mastery over until the dissolution of the Soviet Union. With such a strong position – basically unassailable, with the Red Army built up afresh by massive Lend-Lease aid and domestic production, and honed to a relatively professional force – the Soviet leader had no reason to yield an inch on Poland or the rest of Eastern Europe, and in fact he did not. Roosevelt and Churchill simply had no leverage at all to compel Stalin to restore the freedom of his new client states. They could offer little the Soviets did not already have, and with the Third Reich still actively at war, they could not risk a full breach with Stalin that might (as they believed) cause the two mustached dictators to unite again. Short of declaring war on the Soviet Union and defeating it in an extensive battle, the American and British heads of state had no options to induce Stalin's compliance.

With characteristic astuteness, the translator Charles Bohlen summed up the untenable position of the Western Allies succinctly: "I do not presume to know what was going on in Roosevelt's mind, but from what he said at Yalta [...] I feel that he did everything he could to help the Poles. [...] The compromise failed because Stalin insisted on more than security against attack; he wanted to establish the Soviet system of authoritarian control of every aspect of life in Poland. The Red Army gave Stalin the power he needed to carry out his wishes, regardless of his promises at Yalta. Stalin held all the cards and played them well. Eventually, we had to throw in our hand." (Bohlen, 1973, 192).

One other disadvantage hampered the Western Allies' negotiations. Their accounts inadvertently reveal them, despite their political acumen, as basically honest men. They tended to want to believe the best of Stalin and the Soviets, taking gestures of friendliness at face value. Both, particularly Roosevelt, overlooked signs of Soviet hostility, believing Stalin to be a "good fellow" at bottom, one who liked them and wanted to reach a mutually beneficial understanding.

While remembering expediency and showing skill and even occasional duplicity working within their own democratic systems, they still showed clearly that they came from a relatively civilized political climate. They showed comparatively open and trusting personalities, and a reflexive assumption that their their Soviet counterpart would, to some degree at least, "play fair." Both men had limits they would not pass.

Stalin, the product of a murderous revolution and an even more murderous dictatorship who survived and reigned through treachery, brutality, and terror among the violent, deadly men comprising the Soviet power structure, wielded a cunning his more forthright Western counterparts proved ill-equipped to match. The Soviet dictator had overseen a state founded on mass executions, torture, prison camps, assassination, engineered famine, and the utter dominance of the state over every facet of public and private life. He recognized no limits to his actions; he aimed to win, and he applied all his considerable cunning to achieving this goal.

Furthermore, he hated the two men he dealt with venomously, despite his outward show of friendliness. One of his rants to Yugoslav communist leader Milovan Djilas in 1944 revealed his true loathing of Roosevelt and Churchill as the caricatured representatives of a capitalist system he wholly demonized and wished to destroy: "Perhaps you think that just because we are the allies of the English we have forgotten who they are [...] And Churchill? Churchill is the kind who, if you don't watch him, will slip a kopeck out of your pocket. Yes, a kopeck out of your pocket! By God, a kopeck out of your pocket! And Roosevelt? Roosevelt is not like that. He dips in his hand only for bigger coins. But Churchill? Churchill—even for a kopeck." (Plokhy, 2010, 84).

Finally, it's important to remember that the Western Allies still lacked the powerful bargaining chip of nuclear weapons. The atom bomb remained several months in the future, and even Roosevelt's staff had skepticism that it would ever work. In fact, Truman's decision to drop two bombs on Japan may have been partly an effort to redress the imbalance of power between the Soviet Union and the West inherited from the Yalta Conference. Truman certainly used the threat of nuclear power adroitly a few years later, successfully bluffing the belligerent Soviet Union with a list of 30 major Soviet cities chosen for nuclear annihilation at a point in time when America possessed only 8 nuclear bombs.

Either way, while Yalta represented an overall failure for Roosevelt and Churchill on most matters, the force of circumstance could not make it otherwise. Stalin held the high ground on most of the matters under discussion and, unsurprisingly, emerged with most of the territories and concessions he wanted, since he already enjoyed possession of them.

Churchill tried to save the British Empire and ultimately failed, but Roosevelt did manage one striking diplomatic success in the establishment of the United Nations, a body that has continued to influence global affairs into the 21st century, over 70 years after the Yalta Conference concluded.

The Potsdam Conference

Chapter 1: The Prelude to the Potsdam Conference

Following the Yalta Conference, which produced bombastic declarations but failed to resolve a host of issues about the postwar world, including the disposition of Germany and the relations between the republics of the west and the Soviet Union's dictatorship, the Third Reich fell to the Allies' victorious armies in May. With that, the Empire of Japan, last of the Axis powers, fought on alone, caught in a steel noose of American military power.

Meanwhile, near the end of 1944, as Allied forces were pushing across the Pacific and edging ever closer to Japan, plans were drawn up to invade the Ryuku islands, the most prominent of them being Okinawa. Military planners anticipated that an amphibious campaign would last a week, but instead of facing 60,000 Japanese defenders as estimated, there were closer to 120,000 on the island at the beginning of the campaign in April 1945. The Battle of Okinawa was the largest amphibious operation in the Pacific theater, and it would last nearly 3 months and wind up being the fiercest in the Pacific theater during the war, with nearly 60,000 American casualties and over 100,000 Japanese soldiers killed. In addition, the battle resulted in an estimated 40,000-150,000 Japanese civilian casualties.

Okinawa witnessed every conceivable horror of war both on land and at sea. American ground forces on Okinawa had to deal with bad weather (including a typhoon), anti-tank moats, barbed wire, mines, caves, underground tunnel networks, and fanatical Japanese soldiers who were willing to use human shields while fighting to the death. Allied naval forces supporting the amphibious invasion had to contend with Japan's notorious kamikazes, suicide pilots who terrorized sailors as they frantically tried to shoot down the Japanese planes before they could hit Allied ships. As one sailor aboard the USS *Miami* recalled, "They came in swarms from all directions. The barrels of our ship's guns got so hot we had to use firehoses to cool them down." As *The Marine Corps Gazette* noted, "More mental health issues arose from the Battle of Okinawa than any other battle in the Pacific during World War II. The constant bombardment from artillery and mortars coupled with the high casualty rates led to a great deal of men coming down with combat fatigue. Additionally the rains caused mud that prevented tanks from moving and tracks from pulling out the dead, forcing Marines (who pride themselves on burying their dead in a proper and honorable manner) to leave their comrades where they lay. This, coupled with thousands of bodies both friend and foe littering the entire island, created a scent you could nearly taste. Morale was dangerously low by the month of May and the state of discipline on a moral basis had a new low barometer for acceptable behavior. The ruthless atrocities by the Japanese throughout the war had already brought on an altered behavior (deemed so by traditional standards) by many Americans resulting in the desecration of Japanese remains, but the Japanese tactic of using the Okinawan people as human shields brought about a new aspect of terror and torment to the psychological capacity of the Americans."

Given the horrific nature of the combat, and the fact that it was incessant for several weeks, it's no surprise that Okinawa had a profound psychological effect on the men who fought, but it also greatly influenced the thinking of military leaders who were planning subsequent campaigns, including a potential invasion of the Japanese mainland.

President Franklin Roosevelt died suddenly on April 12th, 1945, survived for just 18 days by Adolf Hitler, and the abrupt death of America's leader after an illness whose gravity his doctors concealed even from him (at his express instructions) made another meeting between the chief Allied leaders – the Big Three – even more urgent. However, Harry S. Truman, Roosevelt's vice president during his final term and the new president by established Constitutional succession, represented a sharp departure from Roosevelt in many ways. Where Roosevelt displayed an elusive, reserved, almost formless internationalism, Truman placed American interests first, last, and always, pursuing them vigorously with a clear, keen mind and determined pragmatism. While Roosevelt preferred delay, vagueness, and uncertainty as policy tools, Truman wanted most things out in the open and tended to say what he thought, unless he saw a reason for keeping his own council, as in the case of the nuclear bombs at the Potsdam Conference. Though the men clashed, his Secretary of State, James F. Byrnes, provided an equally strong dedication to achieving American advantage, combined with a deep, adroit slyness able on occasion to baffle even the slippery Vyacheslav Molotov.

Byrnes

Molotov

While the Americans were mopping up in Okinawa and contemplating the next action, things in Germany were incredibly uneasy in the wake of Hitler's demise and would need to be discussed at Potsdam. The vast armies of East and West met and now shared an uneasy truce along their furthest lines of advance. Vast hordes of German refugees fleeing the mass rape and other atrocities of the Red Army poured westward ahead of the Russians into the comparative safety of the Anglo-American sector. On April 25th, 1945 American and Soviet soldiers met for the first time along the Elbe River.

A Texan first lieutenant, Albert Kotzebue, led a column of seven scouting Jeeps towards the river, marveling at both the swarms of terrified, exhausted German men, women, and children pouring west and at the beauty of the lilacs, tulips, and fruit trees blossoming throughout the landscape. In the village of Leckwicz, Kotzebue's small unit made the first known contact between ground troops of the USA and USSR in Germany. They encountered a lone cavalry scout from Kazakhstan, Aitkalia Alibekov, of the Red Army 58th Guards Rifle Division. This eventually led to handshakes, embraces, and wildly joyful professions of friendship on the banks of the Elbe.

While the reaction on the American side at least initially expressed unbounded enthusiasm for their new "friends," the men soon recognized they came from cultural backgrounds utterly alien to one another. Wariness quickly grew into barely suppressed hostility. Red Army atrocities outraged the Americans as well. While capable of a moderate amount of looting and rapes, the western armies' worst efforts paled beside an average Soviet unit's daily activities in Germany. A Soviet propaganda officer, Georgi Solyus, secretly wrote down what he witnessed: "Looting everywhere. Cars, Studebakers, loaded to the roof with loot. This is wild plundering in the real sense of the term. Women being raped. It is terrible to write this. Primal violence [...] Almost all the buildings are burning. It is dark from smoke and soot. Walls are collapsing, crushing people, but that does not stop the soldiers. They enter the houses like they did before, [...] dragging everything away, dragging, dragging." (Dobbs, 2012, 191).

The Soviet soldiers destroyed practically everything they could not carry off. American soldiers in the Soviet zone noted with astonishment how even towns untouched by battle resembled chaotic garbage dumps. The Russians threw every piece of furniture, item of housewares, paintings, books, lamps, and other possession out of the houses and smashed it to pieces, then slept on the bare floors of buildings surrounded by mounds of shattered rubbish.

Meanwhile, the raping – and the mass suicide of German women attempting to avoid sexual violence or driven to despair by repeated gang-rapes – continued anywhere the Soviets could find women. Rapes by Soviet soldiers in Germany outnumbered those by American soldiers by a factor of at least 100:1 (11,000 to 20,000 women raped by Americans, 2 million women raped by Soviets, some as many as 60 to 70 times individually). German women of all ages attempted to temporarily disfigure their faces with various homemade concoctions in the hopes of making themselves too hideous for the Russians to consider sexually assaulting them.

With men who viewed one another as plundering, raping barbarians on one hand and reactionary capitalist lackeys on the other, the proximity of millions of heavily armed American and Soviet soldiers along hundreds of miles of front presented another issue in need of urgent addressing before fighting broke out among the putative allies.

Additionally, major cracks also appeared among the higher echelons of the wartime Allies. George Frost Kennan, an important American diplomat and specialist on Russian history and culture warned from the beginning that the Soviets would prove a lethal danger. Now, another member of the presidential diplomatic staff, Charles Bohlen, saw that peril materializing before his eyes: "We sent a stream of protests to Moscow, and so did the British. [...] Despite all the messages on Poland sent [...] there was not the slightest sign that the Soviets paid any attention. [...] Poland was just one of the areas where the Soviet Union was acting like an enemy and not like an ally. In Rumania, Hungary, Bulgaria, and elsewhere, the Soviets were showing that the Declaration on Liberated Europe meant nothing (Bohlen, 1973, 208).

Bohlen

Stalin responded belligerently with the accusation that the western Allies' rapid advance must result from a secret collusion between them and Nazi Germany. The normally unflappable Roosevelt boiled over with rage at this calculated insult, firing off a harsh retort which prompted the wily Stalin to backpedal and pass the blame to his advisers with the deftness of a well-practiced politician.

Truman inherited this difficult situation when Roosevelt died. Churchill and Stalin, though familiar with one another, now faced the prospect of negotiating with a man mostly representing an unknown quantity. Roosevelt's death did, however, smooth over one diplomatic wrangle. Stalin earlier canceled Molotov's appearance at the San Francisco meeting establishing the United Nations (UN), but, apparently actually shocked by the American president's death, he agreed immediately to Averell Harriman's proposal that he send Molotov after all as a mark of respect to FDR.

Harriman

With the Allies clearly drifting apart following their victory over the Nazis, Churchill saw the need for a new conference as soon as possible and contacted both Truman and Stalin about the subject. Churchill, in particular, wanted anxiously to prevent the United States from withdrawing all its forces out of Europe, fearing that in the absence of American troops, the Soviets would see no reason to halt and would continue to push forward and take the rest of Western Europe. Churchill, in fact, ordered General Bernard Montgomery to keep the weapons of the 2 million Wehrmacht soldiers who surrendered to the British intact, so that the Germans could be quickly rearmed if it proved necessary to fight the Soviets. He also ordered German military aircraft preserved for the same reason: "No German aircraft in British control which has a serviceable war value, including spares, is to be destroyed by the Germans or by us without Cabinet sanction." (Dobbs, 2012, 211).

Following his contacts with Churchill, Truman sent the Wisconsin-born diplomat and lawyer Joseph Davies to speak with him in June. His judgment apparently failed him at this point if he intended to start his relationship with the British Prime Minister positively. Davies, a man with the soapy manner and appearance of a small-time huckster, repulsed Churchill. Furthermore, unlike the intensely anti-communist Churchill, Davies viewed Soviet communism with something approaching worship. Davies adulated the Soviets, whom he seemingly viewed as heroic figures. Witnessing the grotesque show trials during Stalin's purges, in which victims – coached to confess with beatings prior to their courtroom appearances – made bizarrely excessive confessions of sabotage and treason before being hustled off to the killing grounds, Davies enthusiastically endorsed the judicial murders as fair and considered the executions just. Following this initial meeting with Davies, Churchill called for "a bath in order to get rid of the ooze and slime," (Dobbs, 2012, 221) but he formed a favorable impression of Truman from his letters. The later meeting of the two men confirmed Churchill in this opinion.

Davies

During April and May of 1945, the three leaders and their representatives hammered out a decision to meet and discuss the pressing issues facing them. Everyone sensed a deteriorating situation existed, yet nobody had a complete solution for the problems facing them. The Big Three felt the inevitable suction of future conflict pulling their nations in opposite directions and hoped that the coming conference might smooth out some difficulties.

Once the conference was decided on, Churchill provided it with the name "Terminal" and the two superpowers worked out the details. Stalin refused to hold the meeting anywhere but in Berlin, which lay in the Soviet zone of occupation. Though this soothed his paranoia, it proved destined to give his Western allies an alarming firsthand look at the brutal police state enforced in the Soviet sphere of influence.

Truman picked the date of the summit – late July - to give him sufficient time to prepare. Churchill had preferred an earlier date but found himself overruled.

Thus, the Big Three would gather in Potsdam, a southwestern suburb of Berlin little touched by the devastation visited upon the rest of the Third Reich's capital. The Soviets also found Potsdam festooned with old palaces and manors suitable for housing the august personages about to decide the fate of Germany and the world.

Chapter 2: Potsdam

The American presidential party boarded the USS *Augusta,* a heavy cruiser with an extensive service history both in the Pacific and during the D-Day landings, and sailed from Norfolk, Virginia on July 7th, 1945. In addition to Truman, the vessel carried Secretary of State Byrnes, Soviet expert and translator Charles Bohlen, Admiral William Leahy, European Affairs Division Chief H. Freeman Matthews, and other key personnel.

The USS *Augusta*

Truman spent most of the voyage, which lasted a week, in intensive briefings in order to acquire the most up to date knowledge needed for negotiations. Occasionally, he played a few games of poker with his closest associates, including Byrnes, to relax, but for the most part he spent his time absorbing reams of material about Germany, the suggestions of the State Department, and data about the other Allies, especially the Soviets.

The American ship docked in Antwerp on July 15th, a Sunday, and Truman and his entourage immediately traveled by car to Brussels, where they boarded a four-engine Douglas C-54 Skymaster transport aircraft to Frankfurt At Frankfurt, an escort of tough Republic P-47D Thunderbolt fighter-bombers joined them for the remaining flight to Berlin.

A Douglas C-54 Skymaster

Truman arrived first among the Big Three on the morning of July 16th, and as he toured Berline, he found a sea of rubble strewn with horrors and stinking intensely of corpses. The president later spoke of "the long, never-ending procession of old men, women, and children wandering aimlessly along the autobahn and the country roads carrying, pushing, or pulling what was left of their belongings. In that two-hour drive I saw evidence of a great world tragedy, and I was thankful that the United States had been spared the unbelievable destruction of this war." (Neiberg, 2013, 123).

1,100 tanks and other vehicles of the U.S. 2nd Armored Division lined the road from Berlin to Potsdam, providing a suitably spectacular demonstration of the Army's might and a gigantic honor guard for the new president. Potsdam itself had suffered little damage during the war, thus remaining a beautiful tract of old palaces, gardens, and parks.

The summit itself and the delegates' housing lay within the Soviet zone of control, though large numbers of American military police and British soldiers joined the full division of Central Asian troops stationed to guard Stalin and his guests. The Soviets did not allow the westerners to leave their assigned zones, however. Those who attempted to do so met groups of Kazakh soldiers with PPSh submachine guns blocking their way and refusing to let them pass. Furthermore, the Russians arrested and removed the entire population of the town to prevent them from presenting a security threat – or, perhaps, from informing the Western delegates of Soviet atrocities. Perhaps not surprisingly, the men and women attending with Churchill and Truman expressed some amazement in letters and diaries over a pristine town totally empty of ordinary inhabitants.

Churchill arrived several hours after Truman, on the afternoon of the 16th. He, too, visited Berlin, finding himself struck with pity for the ordinary Germans who cheered him when they recognized him. He visited the ruined Reich Chancellery and even descended into the Fuhrerbunker, strewn with rubble and stinking intensely of rotting flesh. Then he drove on to meet Truman.

The first meeting between the British Prime Minister and the new president proved cordial, and the two men liked each other immediately. As Churchill later recalled, "He invited personal friendship and comradeship, and used many expressions at intervals in our discussion which I could not easily hear unmoved. I felt that here was a man of exceptional character and ability, with an outlook exactly along the lines of Anglo-American relations as they had developed, simple and direct methods of speech, and a great deal of self-confidence and resolution." (Churchill, 1953, 749-750).

Stalin arrived last, wishing to give his allies a day to view the desolation of Berlin. The dictator, terrified of flying, opted to travel to Potsdam from Moscow via train, and the Soviet state pumped massive resources into preparing the way for its generalissimo's travels. Engineers spent weeks reconstructing the rail line to match the wide Russian gauge, enabling their leader to journey through non-stop without switching trains. The Soviet military also assigned 17,000 carefully selected NKVD soldiers to protect the line, while 15,000 Red Army soldiers found themselves posted to the 516 miles of track between the Russian border and Potsdam, 30 per mile, to watch for partisans, saboteurs, or the last vengeful remnants of German units hiding in the countryside. Nine heavily armored and armed trains traversed the rail line, one for Stalin's use, the other eight bristling with NKVD soldiers on the lookout for trouble.

Stalin showed no curiosity whatsoever about Germany on his arrival. He went directly from his train to a massively armored Packard limousine, which drove straight to his quarters. A numerous, well-armed Red Army motorcycle escort accompanied the Soviet leader's car on its short trip to Potsdam proper.

The three leaders and their entourages occupied buildings on the shore of the narrow but picturesque lake known as the Griebnitzsee, in the Potsdam suburb of Babelsberg. While the location offered pleasant views of water and light woodland, mosquitoes plagued the embassies, who discovered the windows lacked screens. The plumbing also worked very poorly, to the dismay of the Americans.

Von Jorges' picture of the lake

Truman's manor belonged a family of German publishers, the Muller-Grotes. The founder of the clan's fortunes, Gustav, had built the house in 1896, but unbeknownst to the president at the time, the Soviet soldiers had smashed most of the family's possessions, beat the current owners ferociously, and raped their teenage daughters repeatedly while forcing their parents to watch. The luckless family finally suffered complete eviction in May.

The Soviets had removed all of the remaining furniture and valuable paintings. At the same time, they installed listening devices in every room and corridor, which functioned admirably; together with similar devices in the British quarters. These "bugs" gave Stalin a complete transcript of every American and English conversation as quickly as his translators could prepare it.

Unaware of the building's provenance, the Americans dubbed it the "Little White House." Truman described the building as yellow and red despite its name, and commented both on its ugliness and the need to provide furnishings in an unorthodox manner. He noted that the German builders "erected a couple of tombstone chimneys on each side of the porch facing the lake so they would cover up the beautiful chateau roof and tower. Make the place look like hell but purely German – just like the Kansas City Union Station. [...] The house [...] was stripped of everything by the Russians – not even a tin spoon left. The American commander [...] caught the Russian loot train and recovered enough furniture to make the place liveable." (Truman, 1997, 50).

The Russians chose the Cecilienhof Palace as the conference venue. The 176-room structure received something of a Soviet makeover prior to the summit. The Russians painted over any frescos they deemed too "Germanic" with gigantic red stars. The NKVD, moonlighting as interior decorators, installed crimson curtains and red-upholstered furniture to continue the theme of scarlet communist décor. As a final touch, Red Army soldiers planted a 24-foot wide star of red geraniums on the front lawn.

A picture of the palace

Each of the three leaders entered by a different entrance and received a third of the Palace to use during and between the plenary sessions. Churchill entered through the courtyard entryway, Stalin through the veranda, and Truman via the front lobby. Each had dining facilities on the spot, removing the need to return to their quarters for meal breaks. The meeting room consisted of Cecilienhof's capacious oak-paneled banqueting hall. Overall, the meeting facilities, just like the living quarters, represented a major improvement from conditions at Yalta a few months earlier.

A picture of the Big Three shortly before the start of the conference

Chapter 3: The Start of the Conference

A startling change in the negotiating positions occurred even before the Big Three had the chance to meet and begin their discussions. On July 17th, the same day that Stalin arrived in Potsdam, a cable describing the first successful atomic bomb test arrived from America. On July 16th, 1945, J. Robert Oppenheimer and others set off a 20 kiloton device known as The Gadget at White Sands Missile Base in the Trinity test. Several observers 6 miles away, who boldly stood outside the shelter in order to better enjoy the light show, found themselves thrown flat on their backs by the tremendous air concussion. Brigadier General Thomas F. Farrell, safely inside the shelter, noted the searing, incredible beauty of the multicolored light thrown by the bomb, and its sound: "It was that beauty the great poets dream about but describe most poorly and inadequately. Thirty seconds after the explosion came first the air blast pressing hard against the people and things, to be followed almost immediately by the strong, sustained, awesome roar which warned of doomsday." (Feis, 1960, 169).

Oppenheimer

The detonation of the Trinity test

The report included several other eyewitness accounts, preliminary estimates of the bomb's force, and other useful information. Though sent to the Americans, they immediately shared it with their British counterparts but kept the matter secret from the Soviets. As it turned out, Stalin knew of the test almost as quickly, though not in as much detail, thanks to Russian spies in the United States.

Even before he had all the details, Churchill immediately grasped the importance of the Trinity test to the summit. He described the situation in his memoirs: "To quell the Japanese resistance man by man and conquer the country yard by yard might well require the loss of a million American lives and half that number of British – [...] for we were resolved to share the agony. Now all this nightmare picture had vanished. [...] Moreover, we should not need the Russians. The end of the Japanese war no longer depended upon the pouring in of their armies [...] We had no need to ask favours of them. The array of European problems could therefore be faced on their merits." (Churchill, 1953, 756).

The insightful Prime Minister saw to the core of the matter instantly. The western Allies had prepared to make extensive concessions to the Soviets, despite their profound (and well-merited) reservations about their Eastern ally's evident intention not to liberate the Nazi-conquered nations of Eastern Europe and the Balkans but to substitute Stalin's brutal police state rule for that of Hitler. Now, with a weapon likely to impel Japanese surrender without the need for an invasion incorporating Russian troops, the Westerners had no motivation to accede to all of the USSR's demands.

Stalin, though a clever negotiator in many situations, knew of the test but still found himself outmaneuvered in one regard at least thanks to a classic "black swan" event – an occurrence impossible to foresee but with a profound effect on the outcome of human affairs. He had promised Soviet aid against the Japanese but never provided it, hoping both to avoid a second front and to use Red Army assistance in the costly invasion of the Japanese home islands as a bargaining chip. Now that particular piece of leverage vanished.

This, of course, lay in the future at the start of the conference. On the 17th, Stalin dropped in on his American guest rather suddenly at the Little White House. Truman took a liking to the Soviet leader, albeit recognizing him as a "little son of a bitch," and Stalin apparently reciprocated the friendliness as much as lay in his character, appreciating the American's tendency to speak his mind boldly. Truman recorded his initial impressions, which he later admitted as "naïve:" "Promptly a few minutes before twelve I looked up from the desk and there stood Stalin in the doorway. I got to my feet and advanced to meet him. […] He said […] that he had more questions to present. I told him to fire away. He did and it is dynamite – but I have some dynamite too which I'm not exploding now. […] I can deal with Stalin. He is honest – but smart as hell." (Truman, 1997, 53).

Truman invited the Soviet leader to stay for lunch, and called on Commander William McKinley Rigdon, the White House's Assistant Naval Aid who provided catering for the event, to provide food for their Russian guest also. Rigdon recalled, "All I could do was increase the quantities of liver and bacon that I had planned to serve as a main course, and of side dishes. Everyone seemed to enjoy the meal, Stalin especially. I recall distinctly how the Generalissimo stroked his mustache in satisfaction over the liver and bacon. It is possible, of course, that the success of this potluck lunch was not hurt by the fact that we also served plenty of vodka, brandy, and wine." (Rigdon, 1962, 197).

Ridgdon

Stalin likewise called on Churchill for a long and rather friendly talk, though with a somewhat sharper edge than that with the American, whom the Soviet attempted to impress favorably.

The early days of the Potsdam Conference resembled the Yalta Conference, with the substitution of some new faces such as Truman's for the older members of the delegations now deceased or on different assignments. The Western Allies formed one party most of the time and the Soviets the other. A number of issues came up and no satisfactory solution could be found, leading the Big Three to postpone them to some nebulous future date, just as the Yalta negotiations had done.

Stalin mentioned a completely new issue that had not appeared on the docket previously – that of Francisco Franco's Spain. The Soviet generalissimo wanted revenge on Franco for his defeat of the communist "Republicans." Attempting to drum up American hostility against Spain, Stalin told Truman that Hitler had vanished and that intelligence sources indicated he might be hiding somewhere on Spanish territory. Truman, however, refused to rise to the bait, and Churchill turned the discussion to other topics.

In order to defang Stalin's wish to crush Spain as a fourth Axis power, the war-weary Western Allies inserted a clause into the Potsdam Protocol that included a strong recommendation to exclude Spain, for the time being at least, from the new United Nations organization. This clause read in part, "The three Governments feel bound, however, to make it clear that they for their part would not favor any application for membership put forward by the present Spanish Government, which, having been founded with the support of the Axis powers, does not, in view of its origins, its nature, its record and its close association with the aggressor states, possess the qualifications necessary to justify such membership." (Feis, 1960, 202).

The Americans also proposed that the Germans be allowed and encouraged to begin self-government on the basis of local, democratically elected councils, and from there be permitted to reconstruct a "free and just" government. The Soviets and British both balked at this initially, until the Americans modified the clause to better exclude former Nazis from government positions. In the same vein, the Allies agreed that for the time being, the Germans would not possess an army, paramilitary organizations, or even veteran's clubs or associations, lest they use these as a method for creating new "fighting leagues" like the SA, Freikorps, or SS.

The Soviets had a particular interest in the remains of the Kriegsmarine, the Third Reich's navy. With limited naval assets of their own, the Russians proved keen to acquire modern vessels from the German fleet, so when Churchill suggested sinking the entire Kriegsmarine, Stalin retorted that the Allies should first divide the ships between them, and that Churchill could sink the English portion if he wished.

Eventually, the Allies worked out an arrangement under which they divided German navy's surface ships as evenly as possible between them, while they sank the submarine fleet (with the exception of 30 U-boats retained for research purposes). The Russians used their portion of the ships for some years after the war, while the Americans, already in possession of a huge, fully modern fleet, used some of the vessels as targets during the Bikini Atoll nuclear tests. The British made use of German minesweepers, crewed by captured Kriegsmarine crews, to sweep the extensive minefields laid in British and other European shipping channels during the war.

While these side issues were dealt with, the main topics of the Potsdam Conference soon emerged during these early days as well, including reparations from Germany to the Soviet Union, and the matter of Poland. The two matters soon grew intertwined, since the Western Allies used the seizure of German territory by Poland as one of a number of important reasons why the $20 billion reparations figure first aired at Yalta could not be met.

A picture of the three leaders shaking each other's hands at the conference

Chapter 4: An Improved Bargaining Position

July 21st, 1945 represented a significant turning point for the Potsdam summit. On this day, a messenger from the Pentagon arrived in the German city with the full 12-page report on the Trinity test. Though Truman and Churchill already knew that the power of the new atom bomb significantly exceeded that of all previous ordnance, the descriptions and figures in the full dispatch proved without a doubt that the United States now stood as the sole possessor of an unprecedented weapon, one capable of ending wars without the intervention of ground troops. After the long-faced, white-mustached U.S. Secretary of War Henry L. Stimson, then 77 years old, read the document to the two Western Allied leaders, both expressed excitement at their much stronger bargaining position. They did not yet envision using atomic leverage directly on the Soviets, but both Truman and Churchill now averred that they would not need the Red Army to defeat Japan.

Stimson

Another key document made an appearance on July 21st. The cunning Secretary of State, James Byrnes, received a decoded cable sent by Minister Togo Shigenori to the Japanese ambassador then in Moscow. This message read in part, "With regard to unconditional surrender, we are unable to consent to it under any circumstances whatsoever. Even if the war drags on, it becomes clear that it will take more blood shed. So long as the enemy demands unconditional surrender, the whole country as one man will pit itself against the enemy in accordance with the Emperor's will." (Robertson, 1994, 431).

The Soviets brusquely dismissed the Japanese peace effort, which had only partial government backing in any case and presented no concrete plan for a negotiated surrender for the Russians to even consider, but Byrnes felt that the message indicated a Japanese intention to fight on. He deemed this would necessitate use of the atom bomb, and, diverging from Truman's opinion, also thought a Soviet-assisted invasion of Kyushu would prove necessary to bring about Japanese capitulation.

Truman, almost always keen to come to the point of any discussion, tackled the question of Poland immediately when the plenary session of July 21st opened. Filled with fresh resolve and the knowledge that he could likely win against Japan even if the Soviet Union sent no soldiers to the Western Allies' assistance, he noted crisply that while he had no objection to three occupation zones in Germany, Stalin now appeared to be unilaterally granting the Poles a fourth zone. Though he left it unsaid, Poland remained under the thumb of the USSR, so the fourth zone effectively represented an addition to Stalin's territorial claims in Germany.

Churchill, suspecting the Soviets of the blackest treachery and considering them apt to roll onward to the Atlantic, backed Truman's position, though the two men actually approached the problem from somewhat different perspectives. In this action, Churchill attempted a sort of damage control. He originally supported giving part of Poland to Russia, and part of Germany to Poland, at Tehran and Yalta. Now, confronted by the reality of the situation, he apparently regretted his earlier choices, seeking to undo them. However, Stalin pointed out his clear agreement at Yalta, remaining unmoved at the report of millions of Germans displaced westward out of the new Polish territories. These people, then believed to number approximately 8.25 million individuals, actually numbered from 14.1-22 million, with another 1 to 2 million killed by the rampaging Soviets or dying on the road.

While the Allies argued over a fait accompli, Stalin also stated he wanted to summon members of the communist-dominated Lublin Government of Poland, installed by the Red Army, to the conference in order to present the "Polish" view. Truman and Churchill agreed, with the Poles likely to arrive on July 24th.

On July 22nd, Secretary of State Byrnes adroitly brought the matter of Poland and the question of German reparations to the Soviet Union together, finally demolishing the Soviet claims to $20 billion in repayments from Germany. Correctly guessing that prostrate, devastated Germany could not offer such a sum and that by default the United States would pay the difference, Byrnes went on the offensive. As Charles Bohlen reported, "Byrnes used strategy learned in the cloakroom of the Senate to force a Soviet retreat. What he did was link reparations to the question of Germany's border with Poland and tell the Soviets they could not have their way on both matters. He said [...] [the] eastern area contained raw materials needed in the western part of Germany. He pointed out, too, that the Soviets had already removed large amounts of German equipment." (Bohlen, 1973, 232).

This negotiation, carried on at the secondary level by Byrnes and Molotov, quickly led to the collapse of Soviet demands on the reparations front. In effect, Byrnes noted that since the Russians already de facto controlled a productive slice of eastern Germany through their puppet Polish state, the Allies now governed too little territory to extract the reparations demanded.

Molotov backed down in a series of retreats, outmaneuvered by the sly South Carolina senator. He first reduced the amount of reparations, then transformed it into an unspecified sum, to be paid in surplus industrial material from western Germany in exchange for coal, food, and other raw materials from the Soviet zone.

The foreign ministers: Molotov, Byrnes, and Anthony Eden

In fact, Byrnes' strategy had the effect of eventually canceling Soviet reparations demands entirely. The Soviets never sent any raw materials or food to the West and therefore had no claim, under the new terms of the agreement, to receive any machinery in exchange. The

Americans worked out this arrangement to avoid impoverishing Germany any more than the war already had. If stripped of all capital goods, food, and other items, the former Reich would become a disaster area, and the aftermath of World War I had already shown such conditions made Germany ripe for the emergence of a new dictator. In fact, the American government ended up providing food to the defeated Germans for the rest of 1945 and into 1946, preventing mass starvation. With between 13.5 million and 22 million Germans expelled from the new Polish territory in the east, and a countryside devastated by war, the U.S. had no choice but to assist the Germans or let them starve. They chose to assist, preventing an additional humanitarian disaster.

The Americans also remained well aware that the Soviets had already plundered large quantities of material from the western zones before withdrawing to their own area, in some cases dismantling entire factories and shipping them east. Thus, when the Soviets asked for a hand in administering the Ruhr industrial district, the British – who held it – refused point blank, guessing that trains full of Ruhr machinery would soon begin rolling east if they agreed. Charles Bohlen even suspected that the Soviets wished to deliberately bring the Germans to pauperage in order to prepare the way for a communist revolution that would promise an end to their misery.

Chapter 5: Impasse

The plenary session on July 23rd, one day before the arrival of the Polish representatives, turned to the matter of Stalin's wishes for partial control of the Dardanelles, the passage from the Black Sea into the Mediterranean. The Soviet leader wanted this concession due to Russia's long-standing desire for a warm-water port. Since the Turks opposed this, the matter appeared to be a potential bone of contention, but Truman opted to support Stalin's idea on the 23rd. In fact, he expanded on it enthusiastically with a pet project of his own, one he believed likely to promote future peace on a wide and permanent scale. The President described his ideas: "The United States Government proposes that there be free and unrestricted navigation of such inland waterways as border on two or more states and that the regulation of such navigation by provided by international authorities representative of all nations directly interested in navigation on the waterways concerned." (Feis, 1960, 298). Stalin, however, showed little favor to that idea, simply stating that he would need to examine the plan in detail before he could even offer an opinion on it.

That evening, Churchill hosted a magnificent dinner for 28 guests at his assigned manor, complete with music, fine food, and innumerable toasts. The British military police managed to set up a truly lordly repast despite the damage inflicted on the building the day before by an exceptionally violent thunderstorm.

For the last time before the Cold War began, the heads of Britain, the United States, and the Soviet Union enjoyed a fully convivial meal together, though Stalin could not resist injecting a note of business by returning stubbornly to the matter of the Dardanelles, to which Churchill responded glibly, "I will always support Russia in her claim to the freedom of the seas all the year round." (Churchill, 1953, 793). Underlining the unexpectedly friendly atmosphere, Stalin rose at the end of the dinner and began collecting the autographs of everyone else present on his menu. The other men appeared nonplussed at the sight of the dictator creating a souvenir, then joined in, until nearly every attendee left with a menu heavy with historic signatures.

The Polish contingent of 10 Lublin officials arrived on July 24th and presented their case at the plenary session that day. Boleslaw Bierut, a much-loathed communist leader and NKVD man who particularly irked Churchill but never failed to flatter Stalin at every opportunity, held forth at length on the need to accept the Curzon Line. In fact, Bierut demanded an even larger piece of German territory, constituting around 25% of Germany's main agricultural region, in addition to large reparations in machinery. During the following days, he and his band of representatives moved between the delegations, presenting fresh territorial demands to any official who would listen to them. Characteristic of each man, Truman had them politely evicted after 15 minutes, while Churchill treated them to a 2-hour session of his oratory.

Bierut

On the 24th, following the plenary session, Truman finally approached Stalin about the atom bomb. He described the weapon in very general terms, and the Soviet dictator, smiling cheerfully, said through his interpreter, "A new bomb! Of extraordinary power! Probably decisive on the Japanese! What a bit of luck." (Neiberg, 2013, 243). Both Truman and Churchill, the latter watching discreetly from the sidelines, thought Stalin failed to understand the significance of what the president told him, but Stalin understood perfectly well the power and significance of the atom bomb. His numerous spies in the United States kept him informed of much of the progress on the weapon and any other data they could uncover. As he had told Molotov early in the meeting, he held the resolve to react as little as possible to the news of any successful test so that he would not encourage Western confidence in the negotiations. Once again, the Soviet generalissimo proved a better poker player than the two Western leaders, and upon returning to his quarters after the party, he immediately telephoned his director of nuclear research and ordered him to increase speed.

The following day's plenary session included Winston Churchill for the final time, though nobody present knew that. The debate proved quite prickly, with the Western Allies confronting Stalin about the brutal police state conditions in Bulgaria, Romania, and other countries conquered by the Soviets. Truman and Churchill also asked for free elections and free press coverage in Poland, along with foreign observers at the elections. Stalin launched a counterattack by claiming the United States and Britain manipulated Italy in the same way. Churchill responded that elections in Italy had been slated for the near future and that the Soviet Union could freely send observers to ensure their fairness, as could any other country of the world. He also used the phrase "Iron Fence," the precursor to his meme-creating statement about the Iron Curtain.

The negotiations on the 25th produced few results. The negotiating parties had reached some of the hard limits of their willingness to compromise, which very closely resembled the actual contours of military occupation on the ground.

The Big Three on July 25

At this point, the negotiations broke off temporarily so that Churchill could return to England for the results of the elections. Following the plenary session, Churchill flew from Gatow Field in German to the Royal Air Force base at Northolt in England for the election of the Prime Minister. The participants set the Potsdam Conference to resume on the 27th. All three of the Allied leaders expected an easy victory for Winston Churchill against his challenger, Clement Attlee. After all, Churchill had just guided his nation to victory through one of its greatest hours of peril.

Churchill went to bed full of optimism and woke on the morning of July 26th in profound despair. Now convinced he would lose, which devastated him with the thought he would no longer be involved in high affairs of state, Churchill went back to bed and only rose at 9 AM. As he now expected, the Labour party had handed his Tories a stunning defeat. Nobody else expected that outcome, not even the Labour Party and its candidate for Prime Minister, Clement Attlee.

The precise reasons for Churchill's loss at the moment of his greatest triumph remain somewhat opaque. Churchill proved a fairly clumsy campaigner, failing to mention the universal health care and other sweeping economic reforms offered by the Tories, while lambasting Labor in excessively accusatory terms. Most likely, the British public no longer saw the need for wartime leadership and wanted a party they hoped would reconstruct the peacetime economy, avoiding the economic troubles of the 1930s. The soldiers voted for Labour hoping for better jobs when they returned home from abroad. The Labour Party had much the same draw at the time as the smaller Common Wealth Party: "The professional ethic and the ideal of service, rather than class interest, were the basis of its appeal [...] managers and workers were to own factories and cooperate in running them." (Thomas-Symonds, 2010, 130).

Churchill, defeated, sank into a brief period of depression, though he still managed a few sallies of black humor, showing he retained some of his customary spirit. In the meantime, Clement Attlee and the new Secretary of State for Foreign Affairs, Ernest Bevin – the replacement for Anthony Eden – prepared to fly to Berlin to take the place of "The Old Man" at the Potsdam summit.

Bevin

While Britain's election results rocked everyone on the 26th, the Allies also issued the Potsdam Declaration, a call for the Japanese to surrender unconditionally, that same day. The declaration threatened the Japanese with "utter and complete destruction" if they failed to surrender. The declaration called for the following:

- "the elimination 'for all time of the authority and influence of those who have deceived and misled the people of Japan into embarking on world conquest'
- "the occupation of 'points in Japanese territory to be designated by the Allies'
- "Japanese sovereignty shall be limited to the islands of Honshu, Hokkaido, Kyushu, Shikoku, and such minor islands as we determine"

- "the Japanese military forces, after being completely disarmed, shall be permitted to return to their homes with the opportunity to lead peaceful and productive lives."
- "we do not intend that the Japanese shall be enslaved as a race or destroyed as a nation, but stern justice shall be meted out to all war criminals, including those who have visited cruelties upon our prisoners."

However, if they yielded, the Declaration outlined the treatment they could expect: "We do not intend that the Japanese shall be enslaved as a race nor destroyed as a nation, but stern justice will be meted out to all war criminals [...] Freedom of speech, of religion, and of thought, as well as respect for fundamental human rights, shall be established. Japan shall be permitted to maintain such industries as will sustain her economy." (Churchill, 1953, 762). The Japanese government quickly issued a public statement in response to the Potsdam Declaration, stating that they meant to "ignore" it entirely.

The new British Prime Minister, Clement Attlee – described pithily by Churchill as "a sheep in sheep's clothing" – failed to impress the other two leaders. Truman disliked him, the Soviet opinion of Attlee quickly sank even lower (though the Briton later naively gave the Russians large amounts of invaluable research on jet engines in a bid to win the Soviet Union's friendship), and even one of the Englishmen present quipped that the Big Three had dwindled to "the Big Two and a Half." Stalin and the Soviets, indeed, expressed both dismay and consternation at Churchill's absence. They could not understand why the British people voted the Prime Minister out of office after he led the English nation through the dark days of World War II to victory. In particular, Stalin expressed his bafflement that Churchill had not simply fixed the result of the election in order to remain in power; the nuances of democracy clearly escaped the generalissimo.

Attlee, who had vigorously supported the "total disarmament" of Britain in 1939 as the only "realistic" way to avert the threat of Hitler, had sufficient good sense to simply confirm the existing British positions at Potsdam. The summit's end approached quickly, and no alteration of such decisions as it made would have had much chance of success at such a late date. Charles Bohlen actually formed a somewhat higher opinion of Attlee: "Until then, Attlee had reminded me of a mechanical toy, which, when wound up and placed on the table by Churchill, would perform as predicted. When he returned to Potsdam [...] Attlee was still his modest, unassuming self, but he showed a measure of strength that I had not seen before. By that time, however, most of the agreements had been made, and Attlee did not attempt to upset matters." (Bohlen, 1973, 239-240).

Chapter 6: The End of the Summit

Attlee, Truman, and Stalin at the conference

The new Prime Minister flew to Berlin on July 28th, causing the next plenary session to occur at 10:30 PM that evening rather than earlier in the day; the original date of the 27th for recommencing the summit underwent revision to reflect the actuality of when Attlee could arrive. At the meeting, Ernest Bevin, who loathed the communists almost as much as Churchill, spoke considerably more than Attlee.

Two out of three of the original Big Three had now vanished from the scene, and the following day, it appeared the last might also. The American and British delegates awoke on July 29th, still adjusting to the strange new world without the bombast, oratory, and humor of Churchill in it, but fully expecting to continue with the negotiations at another plenary session. Instead, an unpleasant and somewhat unnerving surprise awaited them.

Truman and Byrnes sent an invitation to Stalin to meet them at the Little White House for an informal discussion of the situation before the plenary session. Instead, Vyacheslav Molotov appeared and told them that the Soviet dictator, stricken by a sudden cold, could not leave his own quarters that day. The Americans could not fathom if Stalin simply sought to avoid them, perhaps in response to Churchill's absence, or if he had indeed fallen ill and might die. Truman's diary noted his misgivings: "If Stalin should suddenly cash it in would end the original Big Three. [...] I am wondering what would happen to Russia and Central Europe if Joe suddenly passed out. [...] Well, we shall see what we shall see. Uncle Joe's pretty tough mentally and physically but there is an end to every man and we can't help but speculate." (Truman, 1997, 57-58).

Due to Stalin's real or feigned sickness, Molotov and Byrnes took the lead in the negotiations both that day and on the following day, July 30th. Truman avoided the conference during Stalin's absence also. Attlee attended but mostly listened to what the other men said or spoke in support of the existing British positions.

Stalin reappeared at the July 31st plenary session, seemingly in perfect health despite the claim he had been too sick during the past two days to even set foot outside his quarters, and talks resumed with more wrangling over Poland and reparations.

The Allies managed to agree on the need for an international war crimes tribunal to bring the perpetrators of Nazi mass murders to justice. The British – first Churchill, and then Attlee carrying on his policy – argued for Nuremberg as the site of the trials. The symbolic intention would, the Allies hoped, impress itself on the German mind. The Nazi Party's infamous rallies occurred in that city during the years of the Third Reich, and the Allied leaders all agreed to that venue on the 31st.

Despite this agreement, the Soviets set up their own trials in Poland and elsewhere. The fate of Rudolf Hess, Hitler's nominal second in command who flew to England early in the war on a quixotic mission to arrange an alliance between the British and the Third Reich, also came to the surface at Potsdam. His name found its way onto a list of the 10 war criminals selected as the symbolic representation of the rest for diplomatic purposes.

Hess

The Allies also agreed not to dismember Germany, a matter Truman considered particularly important. The American president believed the current war sprang largely from the punitive terms inflicted on the Germans after World War I, and he did not want portions of Germany openly detached to cause problems again in the future. The division of the country into two parts, East and West Germany, represented a de facto dismemberment, but the vast majority of Germany remained united, giving it the necessary territory for recovery and avoidance of Truman's fears on that score. The expulsion of the ethnic Germans from the section of territory given to Poland proved grimly effective in quashing any unrest there, since it created ethnic homogeneity in the new Polish state and consequent relative stability.

The Soviet Union had no qualms in accepting Chiang Kai-Shek's Nationalists in China as part of the postwar order, though of course the Russians scooped off some territorial acquisitions. The Soviets also invaded Manchuria immediately after the Potsdam Conference, and they continued their attack into the Kurile Islands for several days after the Japanese formally surrendered, interested in pushing their borders out as far as possible.

Chiang Kai-Shek

In the matter of Iran, which the Americans used as a Lend-Lease route into the Soviet Union during the war, Stalin agreed to withdraw Soviet troops, to the immense relief of the Shah. Truman also stated his intention to remove all American troops within 60 days to send them to the Pacific Theater, leading Stalin to remark, "So as to rid the United States of any worries we promise you that no action will be taken by us against Iran." (Feis, 1960, 304).

The final plenary sessions on August 1st ended on a terse and sour note. First, Stalin and Truman agreed, and Attlee rubber-stamped, a division of Germany (and Europe) based on the actually existing military frontiers. The Soviet Union kept what it controlled, and the rest of Europe would remain free, with the United States administering West Germany in conjunction with the British until a proper civil government established itself.

Truman raised the issue of his international waterways again, but Stalin abruptly and angrily rejected the idea. In doing so, he spoke the only English words anyone heard him enunciate at the conference: "No. I say no."

Attlee made a feeble effort to assist the royalists in Greece as part of the agreement, since they currently found themselves embroiled in a struggle with communist insurgents. However, he was soon forced to abandon the struggle, with the Greek anti-communists left on their own until Truman came to their aid in 1947. The British Chiefs of Staff told Attlee, "In our view the defence of the Greek frontier must be left to the Greek forces and later guaranteed by the world security organization […] In [the] absence of American troops in Greece we cannot entertain the idea of unilateral British military action in [the] Balkans." (Thomas-Symonds, 2010, 146).

After effectively agreeing to the status quo in Europe, Truman and Stalin parted for the final time late on August 1st. The Potsdam Protocol recognized these facts and stated the need for another summit in the near future, a summit that would never take place. Loathing foreign travel, Truman suggested that the follow up summit should gather in Washington D.C., to which the atheistic Soviet dictator answered, "God willing."

Truman jubilantly escaped Potsdam, which he called "that awful city," on August 2nd, shortly after breakfast. Once more boarding a Douglas C-54 Skymaster, the president flew first to Plymouth in England. Before boarding the USS *Augusta* for American shores, he lunched with England's King George VI on the HMS *Renown*, enjoying the monarch's company. After dining on soup, lamb chops, potatoes, peas, and ice cream, Truman boarded the *Augusta* for the Atlantic crossing.

King George VI

While Attlee flew back to England, Stalin returned to the Soviet Union in his armored train, guarded by his bleak NKVD legions. Once ensconced at his Kuntsevo dacha, the generalissimo gave the order immediately unleashing 12 Soviet armies against Japanese-held Manchuria in the Far East. Atom bomb or not, the Soviet leader had no intention of sitting out the Pacific struggle when he could wrest one final piece of territory from an Axis opponent.

Chapter 7: The Atom Bomb and Potsdam

On the evening of July 31st, Truman saw that the negotiations finally drew towards their conclusion. With only one day remaining in the Potsdam Conference (to the president's immense relief), he prepared written orders to be transmitted back to the United States regarding the use of the first two atom bombs against Japan. He included a terse but clear injunction about the timing of the new weapons' deployment: "Release when ready but not sooner than August 2."

A picture of President Truman ordering the use of the atomic bomb

Truman took some of the Manhattan Project's scientists' ethical concerns into account, but the deadly experience of Okinawa made clear that hundreds of thousands of Americans would be casualties in a conventional invasion of the mainland of Japan. Moreover, the fanatical manner in which Japanese soldiers and civilians held out on Okinawa indicated that the Japanese would suffer more casualties during an invasion than they would if the bombs were used. Pursuant to the Quebec Agreement, Canada and Great Britain consented to the use of the bomb. As a result, Truman authorized its use on two sites in Japan.

Interestingly, Truman did not select the targets for the bombing. He indicated that he wanted military, not civilian, targets hit, then turned the matter over to the generals commanding the U.S. Air Force. Hiroshima and Nagasaki ended up on the bombing list due to their value as Imperial Japanese Navy (IJN) naval bases. This represented as close to a military target as the planners could choose, with two other harbor cities included as alternative targets.

While Truman justified the delay of the deployment until after his departure as a mere desire to avoid needing to "explain" the bombing to the Soviets, it seems likely he also doubted the reaction of the paranoid Stalin. Placing himself and Byrnes out of the unpredictable, violent dictator's reach before such a game-changing event happened probably seemed wise to the canny Truman.

Truman and Byrnes left Potsdam on the morning of August 2nd, immediately after eating breakfast. The president's mood lightened immensely as he began the return to America, a sentiment similar to the vast relief expressed by Roosevelt and Churchill upon leaving the Yalta Conference at the beginning of the year. The truculent, demanding Russians made poor company, and the devastated country did little to lift the men's spirits.

From Potsdam, Truman and his entourage flew to Plymouth, England, where the USS *Augusta* awaited them. The heavy cruiser, which had served as the presidential transport on the way to Europe, now struck out across the ocean in unusually fine weather. Truman watched the latest films and listened to classical music to pass the time.

In the meantime, on the other side of the planet, the U.S. Air Force was gearing up to use the atomic bombs. The primary target for the use of the first bomb was the city of Hiroshima, located in south-central Japan and the largest in the Hiroshima Prefecture. The 509th Composite Group of the U.S. Air Force was created to deploy nuclear weapons, thus given the mission to hit Hiroshima. Lieutenant Colonel Paul Tibbets was selected for the mission well beforehand, and had been training at the remote Wendover Army Air Field in Utah. In the days leading up to the use of the bomb, the Air Force dropped leaflets telling residents of Hiroshima to flee, a warning about half the residents heeded.

On August 6, three planes set off from the island of Tinian to make the 6 hour flight to Hiroshima. Tibbets led the mission, flying the *Enola Gay*, a plane named after his mother that carried the nuclear "Little Boy" uranium gun-type nuclear bomb. Two other planes, *The Great Artiste* and *Necessary Evil* accompanied the mission. All three planes were B-29's.

At approximately 8:15 a.m. on August 6th, 1945, the bomb was dropped from the *Enola Gay*, almost exactly as planned. The bomb missed its precise target by 800 feet, an insignificant distance given the bomb's destructiveness. With the detonation of "Little Boy," the destruction of Hiroshima was far from "little." Japanese officials estimated that approximately 70% of the city's buildings were completely destroyed and another 5-10% were severely damaged. 80,000 people were killed instantly, and another 70,000 severely injured.

With that, the entire world had witnessed the devastation of the world's most powerful weapon, and the Japanese government realized almost immediately that an unprecedented weapon had been deployed against them, due to the instantaneous severing of every line of communication passing through Hiroshima. Expecting a deep emotional reaction, the American code-breakers heard only flatly noncommittal reports on casualty figures and probable weapon strength from the Japanese government. Nevertheless, as events showed, the atom bomb managed to get the notice of Japan's rulers, though only just enough.

In the wake of the attack, a prepared announcement from Washington announced, "The force from which the sun draws its power has been loosed against those who brought war to the Far East [...] It was to spare the Japanese people from utter destruction that the ultimatum of July 26th was issued at Potsdam. Their leaders rejected that ultimatum. If they do not now accept our terms they may expect a rain of ruin from the air, the like of which has never been seen on this earth." (Dobbs, 2012, 350).

Truman received the news about Hiroshima 16 hours later on board the USS *Augusta,* and he immediately leaped up, jubilant, to address the crew. He guessed Japanese surrender was now inevitable, a sentiment the crew shared once he gave them a brief description of the bombing. Cheering and applause greeted the news from servicemen suddenly released from the shadow of a direct, incredibly bloody assault on Japan.

While many others greeted the news with concern or even condemnation, these sentiments generally manifested in those unlikely to die by inches on a Japanese beach or perishing to the accompaniment of gangrenous extremities and facial features, pus-filled buboes, bloody vomit, and decaying skin if the Japanese decided to deploy their plague-carrying flea bombs against Pacific forces (or Los Angeles, via submarine).

Even after Hiroshima, Japan refused to surrender. Instead, the Japanese government instituted martial law within the country to prevent anyone from surrendering. As such, Truman's "rain of ruin" continued. The second site targeted was the city of Kokura, in Southern Japan. This time, a plane called the *Bockstar* was to deliver the bomb, piloted by Major Charles Sweeney.

Luckily for the residents of Kokura, its name would remain irrelevant in the narrative of World War II. The nuclear bombing required the pilot to be able to see the ground, but Kokura was obscured by dense cloud cover on the date of the bombing. Thus, Sweeney made the call to divert to the secondary target, a city farther south called Nagasaki.

There, too, the city was covered in clouds, but a very brief break in the cloud cover at about 11:00 a.m. on August 9 allowed *Bockstar* to drop the "Fat Man" plutonium implosion-type bomb it was carrying. The bomb landed significantly north of its intended epicenter, about two miles to the north and west, in Nagasaki's industrial district. As such, Nagasaki was not as badly destroyed as Hiroshima, but over 40,000 people were still killed.

Since Potsdam, historians and pundits have spilled much ink over the question of whether the Hiroshima and Nagasaki bombs represented a military necessity. Some declare the bombs simply enabled Truman to threaten the Soviet Union by attacking the Japanese unnecessarily.

Most of these arguments use a political rather than historical basis. While certainty in history remains impossible, particularly regarding motives, considerable evidence exists supporting the notion that Truman believed the atom bomb necessary to compel a Japanese surrender, sparing hundreds of thousands of American (and possibly Japanese) lives. Critically, due to ULTRA intercepts and the work of their code-breakers, the Americans possessed a clear picture of Japanese communications and intentions. To their surprise, they heard no talk of surrender in July and August 1945, but only of continued resistance and turning the Japanese islands into a "graveyard" for the Americans. Comprehensive data on massive recruitment blended with reports of many troops returning to Japan from Korea and China to paint a clear picture of a nation turning itself into a bristling fortress prepared to make a spectacular last stand.

The Americans initiated preparations for the invasion of Japan, and an invasion force of 400,000 men began mustering for a November 1st, 1945. All the while, the Japanese commenced massive preparations for an apocalyptic defense of the home islands. The initial invasion aimed at the island of Kyushu and bore the name Operation Olympic. A second invasion, Operation Coronet, would capture Tokyo in spring 1946.

The Army already had a long-standing tradition of statistically analyzing its casualties in order to derive tactical and strategic lessons. The Pacific campaign enabled steady updates to these analytical methods as successive battles revealed relationships between terrain, numbers, tactics, new weaponry, and types of combat and the number of casualties suffered. Records show clearly that the Army, Navy, and Air Force began intensive study of expected casualty figures for Operation Olympic at least nine months prior to Potsdam. These studies therefore commenced when Roosevelt still lived and served as president, and the atom bomb represented a highly secret weapon considered likely to prove a dud by the few people who knew of it. This essentially put paid to the later polemicist claims that Truman created the casualty figures out of thin air as a justification after the fact.

Ahead of the use of the bombs, the fighting on Saipan provided a close approximation of the tactical, technical, and terrain conditions expected on Kyushu. A report prepared on the subject in August 1945 provided a clear summary: "In our Saipan operation, it cost approximately one American killed and several wounded to exterminate seven Japanese soldiers. On this basis it might cost us half a million American lives and many times that number wounded ... in the home islands." (Maddox, 2007, 83).

Nor did the military conduct these studies merely for propaganda purposes. In response to this report on Saipan, the Selective Service began calling up 100,000 men per month, almost double the 60,000 men per month drafted earlier in 1945. An accurate estimate represented an absolute necessity to avoid being caught short with sufficient trained men under arms to successfully execute Operation Olympic.

Declassified Pentagon records reveal Truman received a preliminary estimate of 500,000 to 1 million American deaths in late July 1945, weeks before Potsdam. Apparently dubious of such high figures, Truman submitted the data to his civilian staff for confirmation, which they provided, though everyone involved understood the actual vagaries of combat could cause notable deviation from the estimates. One fact emerged with blazing clarity: the invasion of Japan would cost many more American lives than the entire Pacific campaign had to date.

Evidence from the Japanese side suggests a suicidal samurai defiance on the part of the ruling military against the hated, racially inferior "*gaijin.*" Japan's officer corps showed themselves coldly willing to sacrifice many ordinary Japanese if many Americans could be killed in the process – a sort of national "banzai charge." The nuclear bomb, however, rendered this scenario moot; the Japanese would die, but if they took few or no Americans with them, it made the gesture futile.

Photographs show hundreds of suicide speedboats and hundreds more suicide torpedoes packed into coastal basins, ready to ram American landing craft. Soldiers taught small schoolchildren how to remove the pin from a grenade, approach American soldiers, then release the safety lever to detonate the device. War Minister General Anami Korechika, foremost of the "war party," explained the mentality behind these actions: "[T]here will be some chance as long as we keep on fighting for the honor of the Yamato race.... If we go on like this and surrender, the Yamato [i.e. Japanese] race would be as good as dead spiritually." (Maddox, 2007, 40).

The Japanese air force converted several thousand training and recon biplanes into kamikaze craft in July 1945; due to their fabric construction, World War II radar could not detect them, and a preliminary test successfully sank an American destroyer in late July (Maddox, 2007, 65). New kamikaze pilots received night-flying training for these aircraft.

The Japanese even created special diving suits and mines for a corps of *Fukuryu,* or "crawling dragons," men who would walk on the bottom to detonate explosives underneath American landing craft. The Japanese only had time to manufacture 1,000 of these diving suits prior to the August 15th surrender, though the weapon development report survives: "The Type 5 Attack (Suicide) Mine was essentially a charge of explosive mounted on a stick equipped with a contact fuse. [...] Immediately behind the charge was a floating chamber. The weapon could be balanced so that it was readily handled underwater. Its use was simple. The diver rammed the front end against the bottom or side of a boat. He was, of course, destroyed." (Rielly, 2010, 314).

A Japanese peace party existed for much of the war, but it could not overcome or even seriously challenge the relentless militarists of the war party. The Imperial Japanese Army learned in the 1930s how to use assassination and intimidation to control the civilian government without the need for direct military rule. Even in the teeth of imminent defeat, their iron grip did not relax until the slight opportunity offered by the atom bombs.

Shortly before the Potsdam Conference, the peace party sent an envoy to Moscow with a vague, almost content-free indication they wanted to engage in peace negotiations. The Soviets returned the envoy to Japan with a terse statement that they could not open negotiations when their opponents provided no concrete details of the desired bargaining.

Even following the bombings of Hiroshima and Nagasaki, half of the six-man war council remained adamantly in favor of a self-immolating defense against the Americans. With the argument at an impasse (but with continued resistance representing the default position in the event of no decision being reached), the men took the step of asking Emperor Michinomiya Hirohito to mediate, effectively casting the seventh vote.

Hirohito opted for surrender. The Naval Minister Admiral Yonai Mitsumasa, chief among the "doves," candidly described his surprising satisfaction with the nuclear bombing as a method of wresting control away from the military cabal without the government of Japan losing "face" by revealing its deep internal fractures: "I think that the use of the atomic bomb and the Soviet entry into the war are gifts from Heaven. [...] The main reason I have been insisting on saving the situation [surrendering] is neither fear of an enemy attack nor even the atomic bomb and the Soviet entry into the war. Above all, it is the alarming state of domestic affairs. It is good fortune that we can now save the situation without bringing such domestic affairs into the open." (Maddox, 2007, 44).

On August 14th, 1945, five days after the bombing of Nagasaki, Japan's Emperor Hirohito offered a capitulation and unconditional surrender. Despite some initial protest from Japanese militarists, the war was now definitely over. Hirohito cited the unprecedented nuclear attack as the primary reason for surrender, though the Soviet invasion was also a significant factor.

Even with the Emperor's seal of approval and the threat of nuclear annihilation hanging over the islands, the Japanese military acceded to the call for surrender only slowly and reluctantly. After Nagasaki, the American code-breakers detected no public calls for surrender or even high-level discussions of the matter, since the council occurred behind closed doors.

Faced with continued Japanese intransigence, the military suggested deploying a third weapon – another Mark III Fat Man nuclear implosion bomb, possibly the same weapon dropped under the name *Gilda* along with *Helen of Bikini* in the Bikini Atoll tests of 1946 – then under assembly and likely to be ready on August 16th. However, Truman balked at destroying another city if nuclear attacks could not persuade the Japanese to surrender and countermanded this mission. Instead, the military decided to drop the bomb just inland of the Operation Olympic beachhead to annihilate the Japanese coastal defenses, making a huge breach for the initial American assault to exploit. At this point, the Americans had no idea of the radioactive effects left over and did not realize such a plan would send their troops into a nuclear wasteland, with catastrophic results on the combatants of both sides.

Fortunately for both the Japanese and American soldiers earmarked to do battle on Kyushu's shores on November 1st, it wouldn't come to that. War Minister Anami Korechika, one of the fiercest foes of peace (who believed incorrectly the Americans had no more atom bombs) signed the declaration of surrender on August 15th, then committed seppuku at dawn the next day, unable to endure the disgrace of the "Yamato race's" surrender. Hundreds of other Japanese, including many civilians, would follow him in death, particularly after Hirohito's "Jewel Voice Broadcast" confirming that Japan would yield to the Americans.

Korechika

On August 28, the Supreme Allied occupation of Japan began, and the official surrender ceremony was completed on the USS *Missouri* on September 2. Interestingly, the official end of the state of war between the U.S. and Japan, however, did not come until 1952, with the Treaty of San Francisco being signed on April 28 of that year.

In regard to this key historical issue about the Potsdam Conference, an objective reading of the evidence suggests that the Japanese had little intention of surrender prior to the use of the atomic weapons. Even more importantly, American intelligence found no evidence of any plan except frantically aggressive resistance to the last, despite the availability of voluminous decoded high-level communications. Truman and his advisers could only act on the basis of the information they actually had.

A robust chain of evidence points to the use of the atom bomb as a last ditch effort to compel Japanese surrender in the teeth of samurai-culture intransigence. No contemporary evidence supports the idea that the Japanese might otherwise have surrendered prior to some point well after the physical invasion of the homeland. Such a view only emerges in later polemics.

The atom bombing did not represent a spur of the moment decision intended merely to intimidate the Soviets, nor do extensive historical documents support the notion of the American invasion casualty figures as a *post hoc* justification. While the weapon undoubtedly sent a signal to the Soviets they could not ignore – Molotov, who clearly understood the start of the Cold War, albeit as filtered through the lens of Soviet paranoia, said the new weapon had been "not aimed at Japan but rather at the Soviet Union" (Dobbs, 2012, 351) – this represented a fringe benefit from the American standpoint, without which the bomb would still have seen use against the Empire of the Rising Sun.

Aside from debates over Potsdam's influence on the use of the atomic bomb, most historians agree that the summit between the Big Three at Potsdam proved nearly as inconclusive as the Yalta Conference at the start of the year. Its largest achievement, perhaps, consisted of finally laying the specter of Soviet reparations from the western zone of Germany, ensuring that the nation could recover following the devastation rather than becoming an immediate danger to the other countries or collapsing into a sinkhole of utter destitution that made it permanently dependent on the charity of others.

Aside from that, though, things remained at the kind of impasse that ensured the Cold War would commence. The Western Allies sought to pry the Soviet grip off the countries of Eastern Europe, but to no avail; Stalin and his entire government believed that possession was nine-tenths of the law, and nothing but a shattering military defeat would have persuaded them to return within Russia's prewar boundaries. Initially, the Soviets attempted to support quasi-independent regimes in the Eastern European countries they had chosen to conquer rather than liberate. However, as these failed to fall in line with Moscow's every whim, the Soviets gradually increased their direct control, using the countries of East Europe and the Balkans as colonies which, however austere, assisted in propping up the wheezing economy of the Soviet hegemonic state.

The key question of Poland occupied much of the debate, and showed precisely how little common ground existed for negotiation. The Westerners wanted free elections and restoration of a country victimized massively by Nazi Germany and Soviet Russia. Stalin, with Poland pinioned helplessly in the iron grasp of the Red Army, could conceive of no reason to follow a course that might lose him his new acquisition.

The detonation of the atomic bomb removed the need for Soviet aid for the invasion of Japan, thus depriving the summit of another one of its reasons for existence, though the Soviets entered the war at the last minute to acquire additional territory in the Far East.

In the end, it is perhaps possible to declare Potsdam doomed by forces set in motion long before it took place and continuing long after the end of the summit. The Soviet Union represented a brutal, ruthless, dictatorial power infused with a spirit of world revolution; after all, the Soviets had attempted to penetrate into Germany during the interwar years, halted only by the valor of the Poles and the martial skills of Marshal Jozef Pilsudski. For their part, the Western republics had only supported Stalin's more distant dictatorship due to the necessity of opposing Hitler's forces, which threatened them directly.

With the Third Reich shattered, two utterly incompatible systems of culture, society, and thought met along the new dividing line of Europe, the Iron Curtain. The Soviets had no interest in giving up their hard-won territorial gains for the sake of Western statements about democracy and self-determination, which had no meaning to the overlords of the Soviet police state except as symptoms of Western decadence, weakness, and absurdity.

Thus, it's fair to say the Cold War occurred neither because of the Potsdam Conference nor in spite of it. The trajectory to conflict resulted from the irresolvable conflict between two utterly alien sociopolitical systems. With Churchill, Attlee and Truman on one side, and Stalin on the other, there was no chance the sides could reach an accommodation without surrendering the very things that formed the backbone and sinew of their cultures. As a result, the Cold War developed as an extension of historical processes too profound and too elemental for any statesman – even the dictatorial Stalin – to deflect.

Online Resources

Other World War II titles by Charles River Editors

Other titles about the Tehran Conference on Amazon

Other titles about the Yalta Conference on Amazon

Other titles about the Potsdam Conference on Amazon

Bibliography

Beria, Sergo and Francoise Thom. *Beria – My Father: Inside Stalin's Kremlin.* London, 2001.

Birse, Arthur Herbert. *Memoirs of an Interpreter.* London, 1967.

Bishop, Jim. "Mike Reilly: FDR'S Tireless Protector." *The Milwaukee Sentinel,* July 11th, 1973, Part 1, Page 16.

Bohlen, Charles E. *Witness to History, 1929-1969.* New York, 1973.

Bullitt, William C. "How We Won the War and Lost the Peace." *Life* magazine, August

30th, 1948 issue, pp. 83-97.

Churchill, Winston S. *Closing the Ring.* New York, 2002.

Cray, Ed. *General of the Army: George C. Marshall, Soldier and Statesman.* New York, 2000.

Eubank, Keith. *Summit at Teheran.* New York, 1985.

Franklin, William M., and William Gerber (editors). *Foreign Relations of the United States: Diplomatic Papers, 1943: The Conferences at Cairo and Tehran, 1943.* Washington, DC, 1961.

Ministry Of Foreign Affairs Of The USSR. *Stalin's Correspondence With Churchill, Attlee, Roosevelt And Truman, 1941-45.* New York, 1958.

Perkins, Frances. *The Roosevelt I Knew.* New York, 1946.

Reilly, Michael F., and William J. Slocum. *Reilly of the White House.* New York, 1947.

Skorzeny, Otto and David Johnston (translator). *My Commando Operations: The Memoirs of Hitler's Most Daring Commando.* Atglen, 1995.

Yenne, Bill. *Operation Long Jump: Stalin, Roosevelt, Churchill, and the Greatest Assassination Plot in History.* Washington, DC, 2015.

Buhite, Russell D. *Decisions at Yalta: An Appraisal of Summit Diplomacy.* Wilmington, 1986.

Chamberlain, John. "F.D.R.'s Daughter." *Life* Magazine, March 5th, 1945 Issue, pp. 96-108.

Churchill, Sir Winston S. *Triumph and Tragedy.* London, 1953.

Gardner, Lloyd C. *Spheres of Influence: The Great Powers Partition Europe, from Munich to Yalta.* Chicago, 1993.

Manis, Jim. *The Inaugural Addresses of the U.S. Presidents from George Washington to Bill Clinton, 1789 to 1996.* Hazleton, 1998.

Mee, Charles L. *Yalta.* New York, 2014.

Plokhy, Serhii M. *Yalta: The Price of Peace.* New York, 2010.

Stettinius, Edward R., Jr. and Walter Johnson. *Roosevelt and the Russians: The Yalta Conference.* Garden City, 1949.

Wernick, Robert. *Yalta: Witness to History.* New York, 2011.

Churchill, Sir Winston S. *Triumph and Tragedy.* London, 1953.

Dobbs, Michael. *Six Months in 1945: From World War to Cold War*. New York, 2012.

Feis, Herbert. *Between War and Peace: The Potsdam Conference*. Princeton, 1960.

Maddox, Robert James. *Hiroshima in History: The Myths of Revisionism*. Columbia, 2007.

Mastny, Vojtech. *Russia's Road to the Cold War*. New York, 1979.

Neiberg, Michael. *Potsdam: The End of World War II and the Remaking of Europe*. New York, 2013.

Rielly, Robin L. *Kamikaze Attacks of World War II*. Jefferson, 2010.

Rigdon, William M., and James Derieux. *White House Sailor*. Garden City, 1962,

Robertson, David. *Sly and Able: A Political Biography of James Byrnes*. New York, 1994.

Thomas-Symonds, Niklaus. *Attlee: A Life in Politics*. London, 2010.

Truman, Harry S., and Robert H. Ferrell (editor). *Off the Record: The Private Papers of Harry S. Truman*. Columbia, 1997.